THE
TEMPTATION
TO
EXIST

E. M. Cioran

Translated from the French
by Richard Howard

Introduction by Susan Sontag

The University of Chicago Press

Published by arrangement with Seaver Books

The University of Chicago Press, Chicago 60637
Copyright © 1956 by Librairie Gallimard
English translation copyright © 1968 by Quadrangle Books, Inc.
Introduction © 1968 by Susan Sontag
All rights reserved. Originally published 1968 by Quadrangle
Books, Inc.
Reprinted in 1986 by Seaver Books, Inc.
University of Chicago Press Edition 1998
Printed in the United States of America
17 16 15 14 13 12 11 10 09   4 5 6 7 8 9
ISBN-13: 978-0-226-10675-5
ISBN-10: 0-226-10675-6

Library of Congress Cataloging-in-Publication Data

Cioran, E. M. (Emile M.), 1911–
    [Tentation d'exister. English]
    The temptation to exist / E. M. Cioran ; translated from
  the French by Richard Howard ; introduction by Susan
  Sontag. — University of Chicago Press ed.
        p.   cm.
    Originally published: New York : Seaver Books :
  Distributed by H. Holt, 1986, ©1968.
    ISBN 0-226-10675-6 (alk. paper)
    I. Howard, Richard, 1929–   . II. Title.
  AC25.C513   19981
  084'.1—dc21   98-5161
                                                         CIP

INTRODUCTION

"What is the good of passing from one unten-
able position to another, of seeking justification
always on the same plane?"
—SAMUEL BECKETT

"Every now and then it is possible   to
have absolutely nothing; the possibility of
nothing."   — JOHN CAGE

OURS is a time in which every intellectual or artistic or moral
event gets absorbed by a predatory embrace of consciousness: historicizing. Any statement or act can be assessed as
a necessarily transient "development" or, on a lower level,
belittled as mere "fashion." The human mind possesses now,
almost as second nature, a perspective on its own achieve-
ments that fatally undermines their value and their claim
to truth. For over a century, this historicizing perspective has
dominated our ability to *understand* anything at all. Perhaps
once a marginal tic of consciousness, it's now a gigantic,
uncontrollable gesture—the gesture whereby man indefati-
gably patronizes himself.

We *understand* something by locating it in a multi-
determined temporal continuum. Existence is no more than
the precarious attainment of relevance in an intensely mobile flux of past, present, and future. But even the most
relevant events carry within them the form of their obsolescence. Thus, a single work is eventually a contribution to
a body of work; the details of a life form part of a life-
history; an individual life-history is unintelligible apart from

social, economic, and cultural history; and the life of a society is the sum of "preceding conditions." Meaning drowns in a stream of becoming: the senseless and over-documented rhythm of advent and supercession. The becoming of man is the history of the exhaustion of his possibilities.

Yet there is no outflanking that demon of historical consciousness by turning the corrosive historicizing eye on *it*. Just as that succession of exhausted possibilities (unmasked and discredited by thought and history itself) in which man now situates himself seems far from being simply a mental "attitude" and therefore, it might be hoped, capable of being annulled by refocusing the mind. The best of the intellectual and creative speculation carried on in the "West" over the past hundred and fifty years seems incontestably the most energetic, dense, subtle, sheerly interesting, and *true* in the entire lifetime of man. And yet the equally incontestable result of all this genius is our sense of standing in the ruins of thought, and on the verge of the ruins of history and of man himself. (Cogito ergo boom.) More and more, the shrewdest thinkers and artists are precocious archaeologists of these ruins-in-the-making, indignant or stoical diagnosticians of defeat, enigmatic choreographers of the complex spiritual movements useful for individual survival in an era of permanent apocalypse. The time of collective visions may well be over: by now both the brightest and the gloomiest, the most foolish and the wisest, have been set down. But the need for individual spiritual counsel has never seemed more acute. *Sauve qui peut.*

*

One way of explaining that commonplace of contemporary intellectual historians: the collapse, sometime in the early nineteenth century, of the venerable enterprise of philosophical system-building. Since the Greeks, philosophy (whether fused with religion or conceived as an alternative, secular wisdom) had for the most part been a collective or supra-personal vision. Claiming to give an account of "what is," in its various epistemological and ontological layers, philosophy secondarily insinuated an implicitly futuristic standard of how things "ought to be"—under the aegis of notions like order, harmony, clarity, intelligibility, consistency, etc. But the survival of these collective impersonal visions depends on couching philosophical statements in such a way as to admit of multiple interpretations and applications, so that their bluff can't be called by events. Renouncing the advantages of myth, which had developed a highly sophisticated *narrative* mode of accounting for change and conceptual paradox, philosophy developed a new rhetorical mode: abstraction. Upon this abstract, atemporal discourse—with its claim to be able to describe the non-concrete "universals" or stable forms that underpin the mutable world—the authority of philosophy has always rested. More generally, the very possibility of the objective, formalized visions of Being and of human knowledge proposed by traditional philosophy depends on a particular relation between permanent structures and change in human experience, in which "nature" is the dominant theme and change is recessive. But this relation has been upset—permanently?—since the era climaxed by the French Revolution, when "history" finally pulled up alongside "nature" and then took the lead.

At the point that "history" usurps "nature" as the decisive framework for human experience, man begins to think historically about his experience, and the traditional ahistorical categories of philosophy become hollowed out. The only thinker to meet this awesome challenge head-on was Hegel, who thought he could salvage the philosophical enterprise from this radical reorientation of human consciousness by presenting philosophy as, in fact, no more and no less than the *history* of philosophy. Still, Hegel could not refuse to present his own system as true—that is, as beyond history—by virtue of its incorporation of the historical perspective. So far as Hegel's system was true, then, it ended philosophy. Only the last philosophical system was philosophy, truly conceived. So "the eternal" is re-established once more, after all; and history comes (or will come) to an end. But history did not stop. Mere time proved Hegelianism as a system, though not as a method, bankrupt. (As a method, proliferating into all the sciences of man, it confirmed and gave the largest single intellectual impetus to the consolidation of historical consciousness.)

And this quest for the eternal—once so glamorous and inevitable a gesture of consciousness—now stood exposed, as the root of philosophical thinking, in all its pathos and childishness. Philosophy dwindled into an outmoded fantasy of the mind, part of the provincialism of the spirit, the childhood of man. However firmly philosophical statements might cohere into an argument, there seemed no way of dispelling the radical question that had arisen as to the "value" of the terms composing the statements, no way of restoring a vast loss of confidence in the verbal currency in which philosophical arguments had been transacted. Confounded by the new surge of an increasingly secularized, drastically more competent and efficient human will bent on controlling, manipulating, and modifying "nature," its ventures into concrete ethical and political prescription lagging far behind the accelerating "historical" change of the human landscape (among which changes must be counted the sheer accumulation of concrete empirical knowledge stored in printed books and documents), philosophy's leading words came to seem excessively overdetermined. Or, what amounts to the same thing, undernourished, emptied of meaning.

Subjected to the attritions of change on this unprecedented scale, philosophy's traditionally "abstract," leisurely procedures no longer appeared to address themselves to anything; which is to say, they weren't substantiated any more by the sense that intelligent men had of their experience. Neither as descriptions of Being (reality, the world, the cosmos) nor, in the alternative conception (in which Being, reality, the world, the cosmos are taken as what lies "outside" the mind) that marks the first great retrenchment of the philosophical enterprise, as descriptions of mind only, did philosophy inspire much trust in its capacity to fulfill its traditional aspiration: that of providing the formal models for *understanding* anything. Some kind of further retrenchment or relocation of discourse, at the least, was felt to be necessary.

*

One response to the collapse of philosophical system-building in the nineteenth century was the rise of ideologies —aggressively anti-philosophical systems of thought, taking the form of various "positive" or "descriptive" sciences of man. Comte, Marx, Freud, and the pioneer figures of anthropology, sociology, and linguistics immediately come to mind.

*

Another response to the debacle was a new kind of philosophizing: personal (even autobiographical), aphoristic, lyrical, anti-systematic. Its foremost exemplars: Kierkegaard, Nietzsche, and Wittgenstein.

Cioran is the most distinguished figure in this tradition writing today.

*

The starting point for this modern post-philosophic tradition of philosophizing is the awareness that the traditional forms of philosophical discourse have been broken. What remain as leading possibilities are mutilated, incomplete discourse (the aphorism, the note or jotting) or discourse that has risked metamorphosis into other forms (the parable, the poem, the philosophical tale, the critical exegesis).

Cioran has, apparently, chosen the essay form. Between

1949 and 1964, five collections have appeared: *Précis de Décomposition* (1949), *Syllogismes de l'Amertume* (1952), *La Tentation d'Exister* (1956), *Histoire et Utopie* (1960), and *La Chute dans le Temps* (1964). But these are curious essays, by ordinary standards—meditative, disjunctive in argument, essentially aphoristic in style. One recognizes, in this Rumanian-born writer who studied philosophy at the University of Bucharest and who has lived in France since 1937 and writes in French, the convulsive manner of German neo-philosophical thinking, whose motto is: aphorism or eternity. (Cf. the philosophical aphorisms of Lichtenberg, Novalis, Nietzsche, passages in Rilke's *Duino Elegies*, and Kafka's *Reflections on Sin, Pain, Hope, and the True Way*.)

Cioran's broken arguments are not the "objective" kind of aphoristic writing of a La Rochefoucauld or a Gracián, whose stopping and starting movement mirrors the disjunctive aspects of "the world." Rather, it bears witness to the most intimate impasse of the speculative mind, moving outward only to be checked and broken off by the complexity of its own stance. Not so much a principle of reality as a principle of knowing: namely, that it's the destiny of every profound idea to be checkmated by another idea which it implicitly generated.

*

Still hoping to command something resembling its former prestige, philosophy now undertakes to give evidence incessantly of its own good faith. Though the existing ranges of its conceptual tools could no longer be felt to carry meaning in themselves, they might be re-certified: through the passion of the thinker.

Philosophy is conceived as the personal task of the thinker. Thought becomes "thinking," and "thinking"—by a further turn of the screw—is redefined as worthless unless it is an extreme act, a risk. Thinking becomes confessional, exorcistic: an inventory of the most personal exacerbations of thinking.

Notice that the Cartesian leap is retained as the first move. Existence is still defined as thinking. The difference is that it's not any kind of cogitation, but only a certain kind of *difficult* thinking. Thought and existence are neither brute facts nor logical givens, but paradoxical, unstable situations. Hence, the possibility of conceiving the essay which gives the title to one of Cioran's books and to the present collection, "The Temptation to Exist." "To exist," Cioran says in that essay, "is a habit I do not despair of acquiring."

*

Cioran's subject: on being a *mind*, a consciousness tuned to the highest pitch of refinement. The final justification of his writings, so far as one can guess at it: something close to the bold thesis given its classical statement in Kleist's "Essay on the Puppet Theatre." The thesis that, however much we may long to repair the disorders in the natural harmony of man created by consciousness, this is not to be accomplished by a surrender of consciousness. There is no return, no going back to innocence. We have no choice but to go to the end of thought, there (perhaps), on the other side, in total self-consciousness, to recover grace and innocence.

In Cioran's writings, therefore, the mind is a voyeur.

But not of "the world." Of itself. Cioran is, to a degree reminiscent of Beckett, concerned with the absolute integrity of thought. That is, with the reduction or circumscription of thought to thinking about thinking. "The only free mind," Cioran remarks in one of his finest essays, "Thinking Against Oneself," is "the one that, pure of all intimacy with being or objects, plies its own vacuity."

Yet, throughout, this act of mental disembowelment retains its "Faustian" or "Western" passionateness. Cioran will allow no possibility that anyone born into this culture can attain—as a way out of the trap—an "Eastern" abnegation of mind. (Compare Cioran's self-consciously futile longing for the East with Lévi-Strauss's affirmative nostalgia for "neolithic" consciousness.)

Philosophy becomes tortured thinking. Thinking that devours itself—and continues intact and even flourishes, in spite of these repeated acts of self-cannibalism. Or because of them, perhaps? The thinker plays both roles in the passion-play of thought. He is both protagonist and antagonist, both suffering Prometheus and the remorseless eagle who consumes his perpetually regenerated entrails.

*

Cioran writes about impossible states of being, about unthinkable thoughts. That's his material for speculation. (Thinking against oneself, etc.) But he comes after Nietzsche, who set down almost all of Cioran's position almost a century ago. An interesting question: why does a subtle, powerful mind consent to say what has, for the most part, already been said? In order to make those ideas genuinely his own? Because, while they were true when originally set down, they have since become *more* true?

Whatever the answer, one may guess that the "fact" of Nietzsche has consequences for Cioran. He must tighten the screws, make the argument denser. More excruciating. More rhetorical.

Characteristically, Cioran begins an essay where another writer would end it. And, beginning with the conclusion, he goes on from there.

His is the kind of writing that's meant for readers who, in a sense, already know what he says; they have traversed these vertiginous thoughts for themselves. Cioran doesn't make any of the usual efforts to "persuade," with his oddly lyrical chains of ideas, his merciless irony, his gracefully delivered allusions to nothing less than the whole of European thought since the Greeks. An argument is to be "recognized," and without too much help. Good taste demands that the thinker furnish only pithy glimpses of intellectual and spiritual torment. Hence, Cioran's tone— one of immense dignity, dogged, sometimes playful, often haughty. But for all of what may appear arrogance, there is nothing complacent in Cioran, unless it be his very sense of futility and his uncompromisingly elitist attitude toward the life of the mind.

As Nietzsche wanted to will his moral solitude, one feels that Cioran wants to will the difficult. Not that the essays are particularly hard to read, but their moral point, so to speak, is the unending disclosure of difficulty. The argument of a typical Cioran essay might be described as a network of proposals for thinking—along with dissipations of the grounds for continuing to hold these ideas, not to mention the grounds for "acting" on the basis of them. By his complex intellectual formulation of intellectual impasse, Cioran constructs a closed universe—of the difficult—that is the subject of his lyricism.

*

Cioran is one of the most *delicate* minds of real power writing today. Nuance, irony, and refinement are the essence of his thinking. Yet he declares in the essay "On a Winded Civilization": "Men's minds need a simple truth, an answer which delivers them from their questions, a gospel, a tomb. The moments of refinement conceal a death-principle: nothing is more fragile than subtlety."

A contradiction? Not exactly. It is only the familiar double standard of philosophy since its debacle: upholding one standard (health) for the "culture" at large, another (spiritual ambition) for the solitary philosopher. The first standard demands what Nietzsche called the sacrifice of the intellect. The second standard demands the sacrifice of health, of mundane happiness, often of participation in family life and other community institutions, perhaps even of sanity. The philosopher's taste for martyrdom is almost part of his good manners, in this tradition of philosophizing since Kierkegaard and Nietzsche. And one of its commonest expressions—indicating his good manners or his good taste as a philosopher—is an avowed contempt or distaste for philosophy. Thus: Wittgenstein's idea that philosophy is something like a disease and the job of the philosopher is to study philosophy as the physician studies malaria, not to pass it on but rather to cure people of it.

But whether one diagnoses such behavior as the self-hatred of the philosopher or merely a certain coquetry of the void, more than mere inconsistency must be allowed here. In Cioran's case, his disavowals of mind are not less authentic because they're delivered by someone who makes such strenuous and professional use of the mind. Consider the impassioned counsels in an essay of 1952, "Some Blind Alleys: A Letter"—in which Cioran, a steadily published writer in France, puts himself in the curious position of reproaching a friend for becoming that "monster," an author, and for violating his admirable "detachment, scorn, and silence" by publishing a book about them. But Cioran is not just displaying a facile ambivalence toward his own vocation, he is voicing the painful, genuinely paradoxical experience which the free intellect can have of itself when it commits itself to writing (cf. Plato's 7th Epistle) and acquires an audience. Anyway, it's one thing to make the choice of martyrdom and compromise for oneself; quite another to advise a friend to do likewise. And as for Cioran the use of the mind is a martyrdom, more specifically, becoming a writer—using one's mind in public—is a problematic, partly shameful act; always suspect; in the last analysis, something obscene, socially as well as individually.

*

Considered from one angle only, Cioran is another recruit in that melancholy parade of European intellectuals in revolt against the intellect: the rebellion of idealism against "idealism," whose greatest figures are Nietzsche and Marx. And a good part of his argument on this theme is no different from what we have already heard from countless poets and philosophers in the last century and this—not to mention the sinister, traumatic amplification of these charges against the intellect in the rhetoric and practice of fascism. But the fact that an important argument is not new doesn't or shouldn't mean that we are exempted from taking it seriously any more. And what could be more important than the thesis, reworked by Cioran, that the free use of the mind is, ultimately, anti-social, detrimental to the health of the community?

*

In a number of essays, but most clearly in "On a Winded Civilization" and "A Little Theory of Destiny," Cioran ranges himself firmly on the side of the critics of the Enlightenment. "Since the Age of the Enlightenment," he writes, "Europe has ceaselessly sapped her idols in the name of tolerance." But these idols or "prejudices—organic fictions of a civilization—assure its duration, preserve its physiognomy. It must respect them." And, elsewhere in the first of the essays mentioned above: "A minimum of unconsciousness is necessary if one wants to stay inside history." Foremost among "the diseases that undermine a civilization" is the hypertrophy of thought itself, which leads to the disappearance of the capacity for "inspired stupidity . . . fruitful exaltation, never compromised by a consciousness drawn and quartered." For any civilization "vacillates as soon as it exposes the errors which permitted its growth and its luster, as soon as it calls into question its own truths." And Cioran goes on, all too familiarly, to lament the suppression of the barbarian, of the non-thinker, in Europe. "All his instincts are throttled by his decency" is his comment on the Englishman. Protected from ordeal, "sapped by nostalgia, that generalized ennui," the average

European is now monopolized and obsessed by "the concept of *living well* (that mania of declining periods)." Already Europe has passed to "a provincial destiny." The new masters of the globe are the less civilized peoples of America and Russia; and, waiting in the wings of history, the hordes of violent millions from still less civilized "suburbs of the globe" in whose hands the future resides.

The old argument is given without much transformation at Cioran's hands. The old heroism, the denunciation of the mind by the mind, served up once again in the name of the antitheses: heart versus head, instinct versus reason. "Too much lucidity" results in a loss of equilibrium. (This is one of the arguments, by the way, behind Cioran's expressed mistrust, in "Blind Alleys" and "Style as Risk," of the book, of linguistic communication, of literature itself—at least in the present age.) Et cetera.

But at least one of the old antitheses—thought versus action—is refined. In "On a Winded Civilization," Cioran takes the standard view of the nineteenth-century romantics, and is mainly concerned with the toll which the mind's exercise takes of the ability to act. "To act is one thing; to know one is acting is another. When lucidity invests the action, insinuates itself into it, action is undone and, with it, prejudice, whose function consists, precisely, in subordinating, in enslaving consciousness to action." But in "Thinking Against Oneself," the antithesis of thought and action is rendered in a more subtle and original manner. Thought is not simply that which impedes the direct, energetic performance of an act. Here, Cioran is more concerned with the inroads which action makes upon thought. Pointing out that "the sphere of consciousness shrinks in action," he supports the idea of a "liberation" from action as the only genuine mode of human freedom.

And even in the relatively simplistic argument of "On a Winded Civilization," when Cioran does invoke that exemplary European figure, "the tired intellectual," it's not simply to inveigh against the vocation of the intellectual, but to try to locate the exact difference between two states well worth distinguishing: that of being civilized and that mutilation of the organic person sometimes—tendentiously —called being "over-civilized." One may quarrel about the term, but the condition exists and is rampant—common in professional intellectuals, though scarcely confined to them. And, as Cioran correctly points out, a principal danger of being what he calls over-civilized is that one all too easily relapses, out of sheer exhaustion and the unsatisfied need to be "stimulated," into a vulgar and passive barbarism. Thus, "the man who unmasks his fictions" through an indiscriminate pursuit of lucidity promoted by modern liberal culture "renounces his own resources and, in a sense, himself. Consequently, he will accept other fictions which will deny him, since they will not have cropped up from his own depths." Therefore, he concludes, "no man concerned with his own equilibrium may exceed a certain degree of lucidity and analysis."

Yet this counsel of moderation does not, in the end, limit Cioran's own enterprise. Saturated with a sense of the well-advertised and (in his belief) irreversible decline of European civilization, this model European thinker becomes, it would seem, emancipated from responsibility to his own health as well as his society's. For all his scorn of the enervated condition and the provincial destiny of the civilization he belongs to, Cioran is also a gifted elegist of that civilization. Among the last, perhaps, of the elegists of the passing of "Europe"—of European suffering, of European intellectual courage, of European vigor, of European over-complexity. And determined, himself, to pursue that venture to its end.

*

His sole ambition: "to be abreast of the Incurable."
A doctrine of spiritual strenuousness. "Since every form

of life betrays and corrupts Life, the man who is genuinely alive assumes a maximum of incompatibilities, works relentlessly at pleasure and pain alike . . . " (I am quoting from "The Temptation to Exist.") And there can be no doubt in Cioran's thought that this most ambitious of all states of consciousness, while remaining truer to Life in the generic sense, to the full range of human prospects, is dearly paid for on the level of mundane existence. In terms of action, it means the acceptance of futility. Futility must be seen not as a frustration of one's hopes and aspirations, but as a prized and defended vantage point for the athletic leap of consciousness into its own complexity. It's of this desirable state that Cioran is speaking when he says: "Futility is the most difficult thing in the world." It requires that we "must sever our roots, must become metaphysical aliens."

That Cioran conceives of this as so formidable and difficult a task testifies, perhaps, to his own residual, unquenchable good health. It also may explain why his essay on the Jews, "A People of Solitaries," is, to my mind, the only weak essay in the present collection and one of the few things Cioran has ever written that falls below his usual standard of brilliance and perspicacity. Writing on the Jew, who "represents the alienated condition par excellence" for Cioran no less than for Hegel and a host of intervening writers, he displays a startling moral insensitivity to the contemporary aspects of his theme. Even without the example of Sartre's near-definitive treatment of the same subject in *Anti-Semite and Jew*, one can scarcely help finding Cioran's essay surprisingly cursory and high-handed.

*

A strange dialectic in Cioran: familiar elements fused in a complex mix. On the one hand, the now-traditional Romantic and vitalist contempt for "intellectuality" and for the hypertrophy of the mind at the expense of the body and the feelings and of the capacity for action. On the other hand, an exaltation of the life of the mind at the expense of body, feelings, and the capacity for action that could not be more radical and imperious.

But there is a model for this paradoxical attitude toward consciousness in the thought of the mystics. I mean, particularly, the Gnostic-mystical tradition that, in Western Christianity, descends from Dionysius the Areopagite and the author of *The Cloud of Unknowing*.

And what Cioran says of the mystic, in his essay "Dealing with the Mystics," applies perfectly to his own thought. "The mystic, in most cases, invents his adversaries . . . his thought asserts the existence of others by calculation, by artifice: it is a strategy of no consequence. His thought boils down, in the last instance, to a polemic with himself: he seeks to be, he becomes a crowd, even if it is only by making himself one new mask after the other, multiplying his faces: in which he resembles his Creator, whose histrionics he perpetuates."

Despite the irony in this passage, Cioran's envy of the mystics, whose enterprise so resembles his—"to find what escapes or survives the disintegration of his experiences: the residue of intemporality under the ego's vibrations"—is frank and unmistakable. Yet, like his master Nietzsche, Cioran remains nailed to the cross of an atheist spirituality. And his essays are, perhaps, best read as a manual of such an atheist spirituality. "Once we have ceased linking our secret life to God, we can ascend to ecstasies as effective as those of the mystics and conquer this world without recourse to the Beyond," is the opening sentence of the last paragraph of "Dealing with the Mystics."

*

Politically, Cioran must be described as a conservative. Liberal humanism is for him simply not a viable or interesting option at all, and the hope of radical revolution is something to be outgrown by the mature mind. (Thus, speaking of Russia in "A Little Theory of Destiny," he remarks: "The aspiration to 'save' the world is a morbid phenomenon of a people's youth.")

It may be relevant to recall that Cioran was born (in 1911) in Rumania, virtually all of whose distinguished expatriate intellectuals have been either apolitical or overtly reactionary; and that his only other book, besides the five collections of essays, is an edition of the writings of de Maistre (published in 1957), for which he wrote the introduction and selected the texts.* While he never develops anything like an explicit theology of counter-revolution in the manner of de Maistre, those arguments seem close to Cioran's tacit position. Like de Maistre, Donoso Cortés, and, more recently, Eric Voegelin, Cioran possesses—but, again, viewed from only one angle—what might be described as a right-wing "Catholic" sensibility. The modern habit of fomenting revolutions against the established social order in the name of justice and equality is dismissed as a kind of childish fanaticism, much as an old Cardinal might regard the activities of some uncouth millenarian sect. Within the same framework, one can locate Cioran's description of Marxism as "that sin of optimism," and his stand against the Enlightenment ideals of "tolerance" and freedom of thought. (It's perhaps worth noting, too, that Cioran is the son of a Greek Orthodox priest.)

Yet while Cioran projects a recognizable political stance (though it's present only implicitly in most of the essays), his approach is not, in the end, grounded in a religious commitment. Whatever his political-moral sympathies have in common with the right-wing Catholic sensibility, Cioran himself, as I have already said, is committed to the para-

---

* He has also published an essay on Machiavelli and one on St. John Perse—both as yet uncollected.

doxes of an atheist theology. Faith itself, he argues, solves nothing.

*

Perhaps what prevents Cioran from making the commitment, even in a secular form, to something like the Catholic theology of order is the fact that he understands too well and shares too many of the spiritual presuppositions of the Romantic movement. Critic of left-wing revolution that he may be, and a slightly snobbish analyst of the fact "that rebellion enjoys an undue privilege among us," Cioran cannot disavow the lesson that "almost all our discoveries are due to our violences, to the exacerbations of our instability." Thus, alongside the conservative implications of some of the essays, with their scornful treatment of the phenomenology of uprootedness, one must set the ironic-positive attitude toward rebellion in "Thinking Against Oneself," an essay which concludes with the admonition that, "since the Absolute corresponds to a meaning we have not been able to cultivate, let us surrender to all rebellions: they will end by turning against themselves, against us . . ."

Cioran is clearly unable to withhold admiration from what is extravagant, willful, extreme—one example of which is the extravagant, willful *askesis* of the great Western mystics. Another is the fund of extremity stored up in the experience of the great madmen. "We derive our vitality from our store of madness," he writes in "The Temptation to Exist." Yet, in the essay on the mystics, he speaks of "our capacity to fling ourselves into a madness that is *not sacred*. In the unknown, we can go as far as the saints, without making use of their means. It will be enough for us to constrain reason to a long silence."

*

What makes Cioran's position not truly a conservative one in the modern sense is that his is, above all, an aristocratic stance. See, for only one illustration of the resources of this stance, his brilliant essay, "Beyond the Novel," in which the novel is eloquently and persuasively condemned, in the end, for its spiritual vulgarity—for its devotion to what Cioran calls "destiny in lower case."

Throughout Cioran's writings, what is being posed is the problem of *spiritual good taste*. Avoiding vulgarity and the dilution of the self is, needless to say, the prerequisite for the arduous double task of maintaining an intact self which one is able fully to affirm and yet, at the same time, transcend. Cioran's chief accusation against the emotion of self-pity, for instance, is that the person who indulges in it has, by rejecting his miseries and relegating them outside his nature, "ceased to communicate with his life, which he turns into an object." It may seem outrageous when Cioran writes, as he often does, of resisting the vulgar temptation to be happy and of the "impasse of happiness." But such judgments are far from an unfeeling affectation, once one grants his impossible project: "to be *nowhere*, when no external condition obliges you to do so . . . to extricate yourself from the world—what a labor of abolition!"

More realistically, perhaps the best to be hoped for is a series of situations, a life, a milieu, which leave part of the venturesome consciousness free for its labors. One may recall Cioran's description of Spain, in "A Little Theory of Destiny": "They live in a kind of melodious asperity, a *tragic non-seriousness*, which saves them from vulgarity, from happiness, and from success."

Certainly, Cioran's writings suggest, the role of the writer isn't likely to provide this kind of spiritual leverage. In "Advantages of Exile" and the brief "Verbal Demiurgy," he describes how the vocation of literature, particularly that of the poet, creates insurmountable conditions of inauthenticity. One may suffer, but when one deposits this suffering in literature the result is "an accumulation of confusions, an inflation of horrors, of *frissons* that *date*. One cannot keep renewing Hell, whose very character is monotony . . ."

Whether the vocation of the philosopher is any less compromised can hardly be proved. (Reason is dying, Cioran says in "Style as Risk," in both philosophy and art.) But at least philosophy, I imagine Cioran feels, maintains somewhat higher standards of decorum. Untempted by the same kind of fame or emotional rewards that can descend on the poet, perhaps the philosopher, a little better than the poet, can comprehend and respect the modesty of the inexpressible.

*

When Cioran describes Nietzsche's philosophy as "a sum of attitudes"—mistakenly scrutinized by scholars for the constants that the philosopher has rejected—it's clear that he accepts the Nietzschean standard, with its critique of "truth" as system and consistency, as his own.

In "Blind Alleys," Cioran speaks of "the stupidities inherent in the cult of truth."

The implication, here and elsewhere, is that what the true philosopher says is not something "true" but rather something necessary or liberating. For "the truth" is identified with depersonalization.

Once again, the line from Nietzsche to Cioran cannot be overemphasized. And, in the case of both writers, the critique of "truth" is intimately connected with the attitude toward "history."

Thus, one cannot understand Nietzsche's questioning of the value of truth in general and of the usefulness of historical truth in particular without grasping the link between the two notions. Nietzsche doesn't reject historical thinking because it is false. On the contrary, it must be rejected because it is true—a debilitating truth that has to be overthrown to allow a more inclusive orientation for human consciousness.

As Cioran says in "The Temptation to Exist": "History is merely an inessential mode of being, the most effective form of our infidelity to ourselves, a metaphysical refusal." And, in "Thinking Against Oneself," he refers to "history, man's aggression against himself."

*

Granted that the stamp of Nietzsche is to be found both upon the form of Cioran's thinking as well as on his principal attitudes, he most resembles Nietzsche in his temperament. It's the temperament or personal style shared with Nietzsche that explains the connections, in Cioran's work, between such disparate materials as: the emphasis on the strenuousness of an ambitious spiritual life; the project of self-mastery through "thinking against oneself"; the recurrent Nietzschean thematics of strength versus weakness, health versus sickness; the savage and sometimes shrill deployment of irony (quite different from the near-systematic, dialectical interplay of irony and seriousness to be found in Kierkegaard's writings); the preoccupation with the struggle against banality and boredom; the ambivalent attitude toward the poet's vocation; the seductive, but always finally resisted, lure of religious consciousness; and, of course, the hostility toward history and to most aspects of "modern" life.

What's missing in Cioran's work is anything parallel to Nietzsche's heroic effort to surmount nihilism (the doctrine of eternal recurrence).

And where Cioran most differs from Nietzsche is in not following Nietzsche's critique of Platonism. Contemptuous of history, yet haunted by time and mortality, Nietzsche still refused anything that harked back to the rhetoric established by Plato for going beyond time and death; and indeed worked hard at exposing what he thought essentially fraudulent and bad faith in the Platonic intellectual transcendence. Cioran, apparently, hasn't been convinced by Nietzsche's arguments. All the venerable Platonic dualisms reappear in Cioran's writings, essential links of his argument, used with no more than an occasional hint of ironic reserve. One finds time versus eternity, mind versus body, spirit versus matter; and the more modern ones, too: life versus Life, and being versus existence. How seriously these dualisms are intended is hard to decide.

Could one approach the Platonist machinery in Cioran's thought as an aesthetic code? Or, alternatively, as a kind of moral therapy? But Nietzsche's critique of Platonism would still apply, and remain still unanswered.

*

The only figure in the world of Anglo-American letters embarked on a theoretical enterprise comparable in intellectual power and scope to Cioran's is John Cage.

Also a thinker in the post- and anti-philosophical tradition of broken, aphoristic discourse, Cage shares with Cioran a revulsion against "psychology" and against "history" and a commitment to a radical transvaluation of values. But while comparable in range, interest, and energy to Cioran's, Cage's thought mainly offers the most radical contrast to it. From what must be assumed to be the grossest difference of temperament, Cage envisages a world in which most of Cioran's problems and tasks simply don't exist. Cioran's universe of discourse is preoccupied with the themes of sickness (individual and social), impasse, suffering, mortality. What his essays offer is diagnosis and, if not outright therapy, at least a manual of spiritual good taste through which one might be helped to keep one's life from being turned into an object, a thing. Cage's universe of discourse —no less radical and spiritually ambitious than Cioran's— refuses to admit most of these themes.

In contrast to Cioran's unrelenting elitism, Cage envisages

a totally democratic world of the spirit, a world of "natural activity" in which "it is understood that everything is clean: there is no dirt." In contrast to Cioran's baroque standards of good and bad taste in intellectual and moral matters, Cage clearly believes that there's no such thing as good or bad taste. In contrast to Cioran's vision of error and decline and (possible) redemption of one's acts, Cage proposes the perennial possibility of errorless behavior, if only we will allow it to be so. "Error is a fiction, has no reality in fact. Errorless music is written by not giving a thought to cause and effect. Any other kind of music always has mistakes in it. In other words, there is no split between spirit and matter." And elsewhere in the same book from which all these quotes are taken, *Silence:* "How can we speak of error when it is understood 'psychology never again'?" In contrast to Cioran's goal of infinite adaptability and intellectual agility (how to find the correct vantage point, the right place to stand in a treacherous world), Cage proposes for our experience a world in which it's never preferable to do other than we are doing or be elsewhere than we are. "It is only irritating," he says, "to think one would like to be somewhere else. Here we are now."

What is striking, in the context of this comparison. is how devoted Cioran is to the *will* and its capacity to transform the world. Compare Cage's: "Do you only take the position of doing nothing, and things will of themselves become transformed." What different views can be entailed by the radical rejection of history is easily seen by thinking first of Cioran and then of Cage, who writes: "To be & be the present. Would it be a repetition? Only if we thought we owned it, but since we don't, it is free & so are we."

Reading Cage, one becomes aware how much Cioran is still confined within the premises of the historicizing consciousness; how inescapably he continues to repeat these gestures, much as he longs to transcend them. Of necessity, then, Cioran's thought is halfway between anguished reprise of these gestures and a genuine transvaluation of them. Perhaps, for a unified transvaluation, one must look to those thinkers, like Cage, who—whether from spiritual strength or spiritual insensitivity is, to speak bluntly, a secondary issue—are able to jettison far more of the inherited anguish and complexity of this civilization. Cioran's fierce, tensely argued speculations sum up brilliantly the decaying urgencies of "Western" thought, but offer no relief from them beyond the considerable satisfactions of the understanding. Relief, of course, is scarcely Cioran's intention. His aim is diagnosis. For relief, it may be that one must abandon the pride of knowing and feeling so much—a local pride that has cost everyone hideously by now.

*

Novalis wrote that "philosophy is properly Home-sickness; the wish to be everywhere at home." If the human mind can be everywhere at home, it must in the end give up its local "European" pride, and something else—that will seem strangely unfeeling and intellectually simplistic—must be allowed in. "All that is necessary," says Cage with his own devastating irony, "is an empty space of time and letting it act in its magnetic way."

SUSAN SONTAG

THE
TEMPTATION
TO
EXIST

THINKING AGAINST
ONESELF

ALMOST all our discoveries are due to our violences, to the
exacerbation of our instability. Even God, insofar as He
interests us—it is not in our innermost selves that we discern God, but at the extreme limits of our fever, at the very
point where, our rage confronting His, a shock results, an
encounter as ruinous for Him as for us. Blasted by the curse
attached to acts, the man of violence forces his nature, rises
above himself only to relapse, an aggressor, followed by his
enterprises, which come to punish him for having instigated
them. Every work turns against its author: the poem will
crush the poet, the system the philosopher, the event the
man of action. Destruction awaits anyone who, answering
to his vocation and fulfilling it, exerts himself within history;
only the man who sacrifices every gift and talent escapes:
released from his humanity, he may lodge himself in Being.
If I aspire to a metaphysical career, I cannot, at any price,
retain my identity: whatever residue I retain must be liqui-
dated; if, on the contrary, I assume a historical role, it is my
responsibility to exasperate my faculties until I explode along

with them. One always perishes by the self one assumes: to bear a name is to claim an exact mode of collapse.

Faithful to his appearances, the man of violence is not discouraged, he starts all over again, and persists, since he cannot exempt himself from suffering. His occasional efforts to destroy others are merely a roundabout route to his own destruction. Beneath his self-confidence, his braggadocio, lurks a fanatic of disaster. Hence it is among the violent that we meet the enemies of themselves. And we are all violent— men of anger who, having lost the key of quietude, now have access only to the secrets of laceration.

Instead of letting it erode us gradually, we decided to go time one better, to add to its moments *our own*. This new time grafted onto the old one, this time elaborated and projected, soon revealed its virulence: objectivized, it became history, a monster we have called up against ourselves, a fatality we cannot escape, even by recourse to the formulas of passivity, the recipes of wisdom.

Try as we will to take the "cure" of ineffectuality; to meditate on the Taoist fathers' doctrine of submission, of withdrawal, of a sovereign absence; to follow, like them, the course of consciousness once it ceases to be at grips with the world and weds the form of things as water does, their favorite element—we shall never succeed. They scorn both our curiosity and our thirst for suffering; in which they differ from the mystics, and especially from the medieval ones, so apt to recommend the virtues of the hair shirt, the scourge, insomnia, inanition, and lament.

"A life of intensity is contrary to the Tao," teaches Lao Tse, a normal man if ever there was one. But the Christian virus torments us: heirs of the flagellants, it is by refining our excruciations that we become conscious of ourselves. Is religion declining? We perpetuate its extravagances, as we perpetuate the macerations and the cell-shrieks of old, our will to suffer equaling that of the monasteries in their hey-day. If the Church no longer enjoys a monopoly on hell, it has nonetheless riveted us to a chain of sighs, to the cult of the ordeal, of blasted joys and jubilant despair.

The mind, as well as the body, pays for "a life of intensity." Masters in the art of thinking against oneself, Nietzsche, Baudelaire, and Dostoevsky have taught us to side with our dangers, to broaden the sphere of our diseases, to acquire existence by division from our being. And what for the great Chinaman was a symbol of failure, a proof of imperfection, constitutes for us the sole mode of possessing, of making contact with ourselves.

"If a man loves nothing, he will be invulnerable" (Chuang Tse). A maxim as profound as it is invalid. The apogee of indifference—how attain it, when our very apathy is tension, conflict, aggression? No sage among *our* ancestors, but malcontents, triflers, fanatics whose disappointments or excesses we must continue.

According to our Chinese again, only the detached mind penetrates the essence of the Tao; the man of passion perceives only its effects: the descent to the depths demands silence, the suspension of our vibrations, indeed of our faculties. But is it not revealing that our aspiration to the absolute is expressed in terms of activity, of combat, that a Kierkegaard calls himself a "knight of Faith" and that a Pascal is nothing but a pamphleteer? We attack and we struggle; therefore we know only the effects of the Tao. Further, the failure of Quietism, that European equivalent of Taoism, tells the story of our possibilities, our prospects.

The apprenticeship to passivity—I know nothing more contrary to our habits. (The modern age begins with two hysterics: Don Quixote and Luther.) If we *make time*, produce and elaborate it, we do so out of our repugnance to the hegemony of essence and to the contemplative submission it presupposes. Taoism seems to me wisdom's first and last word: yet I resist it, my instincts reject it, as they refuse to *endure* anything—the heredity of revolt is too much for us. Our disease? Centuries of attention to time, the idolatry of becoming. What recourse to China or India will heal us?

There are certain forms of wisdom and deliverance which we can neither grasp from within nor transform into our daily substance, nor even frame in a theory. Deliverance, if we insist upon it, must proceed from ourselves: no use seeking it elsewhere, in a ready-made system or in some Oriental doctrine. Yet this is often what happens in many a mind avid, as we say, for an absolute. But such wisdom is fraudulent, such deliverance merely dupery. I am indicting not only theosophy and its adepts, but all those who adopt truths incompatible with their nature. More than one such man has an Instant India and supposes he has plumbed its secrets, when nothing—neither his character nor his training nor his anxieties—prepares him for any such thing. What a swarm of the pseudo-"delivered" stares down at us from the pinnacle of their salvation! Their conscience is clear—do they not claim to locate themselves *above* their actions? An intolerable swindle. They aim, further, so high that any conventional religion seems to them a family prejudice by which their "metaphysical mind" cannot be satisfied. To convert to *India*, doubtless that is more satisfying. But they forget that India postulates the agreement of idea and act, the identity of salvation and renunciation. When one possesses a "metaphysical mind," such trifles are scarcely worth one's concern.

After so much imposture, so much fraud, it is comforting to contemplate a beggar. He, at least, neither lies nor lies to himself: his doctrine, if he has one, he embodies; work he dislikes, and he proves it; wanting to possess nothing, he cultivates his impoverishment, the condition of his freedom. His thought is resolved into his being and his being into his thought. He *has* nothing, he *is* himself, he endures: to live on a footing with eternity is to live from day to day, from hand to mouth. Thus, for him, other men are imprisoned in illusion. If he depends on them, he takes his revenge by studying them, a specialist in the underbelly of "noble" sentiments. His sloth, of a very rare quality, truly "delivers" him from a world of fools and dupes. About renunciation he knows more than many of your esoteric works. To be convinced of this, you need only walk out into the street . . . But you prefer the texts that teach mendicancy. Since no practical consequence accompanies your meditations, it will not be surprising that the merest bum is worth more than you . . . Can we conceive a Buddha faithful to his truths *and* to his palace? One is not "delivered-alive" and still a landowner. I reject the generalization of the lie, I repudiate those who exhibit their so-called "salvation" and prop it with a doctrine which does not emanate from themselves. To unmask them, to knock them off the pedestal they have hoisted themselves on, to hold them up to scorn is a campaign no one should remain indifferent to. For at any price we must keep those who have too clear a conscience from living and dying in peace.

*

When at every turn you confront us with "the absolute," you affect a profound, inaccessible little ogle, as if you were at grips with a remote world, in a light, a darkness all your own, masters of a realm to which nothing outside of yourselves can gain access. You grant us other mortals a few scraps of the great discoveries you have just made, a few vestiges of your prospecting. But all your labors result in no more than this: you murmur one poor word, the fruit of your reading, of your learned frivolity, of your bookish void, your borrowed anguish.

The Absolute—all our efforts come down to undermining the sensibility which leads to the absolute. Our wisdom (or rather our unwisdom) repudiates it; relativists, we look for our equilibrium not in eternity but in time. The *evolving absolute*, Hegel's heresy, has become our dogma, our tragic orthodoxy, the philosophy of our *reflexes*. Anyone who supposes he can avoid it is either boasting or blind. Stuck with appearances, we keep espousing an incomplete wisdom, half-fantasy and half-foolishness. If India, to quote Hegel again, represents "the dream of the infinite Spirit," the turn of our intellect, as of our sensibility, obliges us to conceive of a Spirit *incarnate*, limited to historical processes, embracing not the world but the world's *moments*, a faceted time which we escape only by fits and starts, and only when we betray our appearances.

The sphere of consciousness shrinks in action; no one who acts can lay claim to the universal, for to act is to cling to the properties of being at the expense of being itself, to a form of reality to reality's detriment. The degree of our liberation is measured by the quantity of undertakings from which we are emancipated, as by our capacity to convert any object into a non-object. But it is meaningless to speak of liberation apropos of a hurried humanity which has forgotten that we cannot reconquer life nor revel in it without having first abolished it.

We breathe too fast to be able to grasp things in themselves or to expose their fragility. Our panting postulates and distorts them, creates and disfigures them, and binds us to them. I bestir myself, therefore I emit a world as suspect as my speculation which justifies it; I espouse movement, which changes me into a generator of being, into an artisan of fictions, while my cosmogonic verve makes me forget that, led on by the whirlwind of *acts*, I am nothing but an acolyte of time, an agent of decrepit universes.

Gorged on sensations and on their corollary—becoming, we are "undelivered" by inclination and by principle, sentenced by choice, stricken by the fever of the visible, rummaging in surface enigmas of a piece with our bewilderment and our trepidation.

If we would regain our freedom, we must shake off the burden of sensation, no longer react to the world by our senses, break our bonds. For all sensation is a bond, pleasure as much as pain, joy as much as misery. The only free mind is the one that, pure of all intimacy with beings or objects, plies its own vacuity.

To resist happiness—the majority manages that; suffering is much more insidious. Have you ever tasted it? You will never be sated once you have, you will pursue it greedily and preferably where it does not exist, you will project it there since without it everything seems futile to you, drab. Wherever there is suffering, it exhausts mystery or renders it luminous. The savor and solution of things, accident and obsession, caprice and necessity—suffering will make you love·*appearance* in whatever is most powerful, most lasting, and truest, and will tie you to itself forever, for "intense" by nature, it is, like any "intensity," a servitude, a subjection. The soul unfettered, the soul indifferent and void— how *in the world* achieve that? How conquer absence, the freedom of absence? Such freedom will never figure among our *mores*, any more than "the dream of the infinite Spirit."

To identify oneself with an alien doctrine, one must adopt it without restrictions: what is the use of acknowledging the truths of Buddhism and of rejecting transmigration, the very basis of the idea of renunciation? Of assenting to the Vedanta, of accepting the unreality of appearances and then behaving as if appearances existed? An inconsistency inevitable for any mind raised in the cult of phenomena. For it must be admitted: we have *the phenomenon* in our blood. We may scorn it, abhor it, it is nonetheless our patrimony, our capital of contortions, the symbol of our hysteria here on earth. A race of convulsionaries, at the center of a cosmic farce, we have imprinted on the universe the stigmata of our history and shall never be capable of that illumination which lets us die in peace. It is by our works, not by our silences, that we have chosen to disappear:

our future may be read in our features, in the grimaces of agonized and busy prophets. The smile of the Buddha, that smile which overhangs the world, does not elucidate our faces. At best, we conceive happiness; never felicity, prerogative of civilizations based on the idea of salvation, on the refusal to savor one's sufferings, to revel in them; but, sybarites of suffering, scions of a masochistic tradition, which of us would hesitate between the Benares sermon and Baudelaire's *Heautontimoroumenos?* "I am both wound and knife"—that is our absolute, our eternity.

As for our redeemers, come among us for our greater harm, we love the noxiousness of their hopes and their remedies, their eagerness to favor and exalt our ills, the venom that infuses their "lifegiving" words. To them we owe our expertise in a suffering that has no exit. To what temptations, to what extremities does lucidity lead! Shall we desert it now to take refuge in unconsciousness? Anyone can escape into sleep, we are all geniuses when we dream, the butcher the poet's equal there. But our perspicacity cannot bear that such a marvel should endure, nor that inspiration should be brought within everyone's grasp; daylight strips us of the night's gifts. Only the madman enjoys the privilege of passing smoothly from a nocturnal to a daylight existence: no distinction between his dreams and his waking. He has renounced our reason, as the beggar has renounced our belongings. Both have found a way that leads beyond suffering and solved all our problems; hence they remain examples we cannot follow, saviors without adepts.

Even as we ransack our own diseases, those of other people regard us no less. In an age of biographies, no one bandages his wounds without our attempting to lay them bare, to expose them to broad daylight; if we fail, we turn away, disappointed. And even he who ended on the cross— it is not because he suffered *for us* that he still counts for something in our eyes, but because he *suffered* and uttered several lamentations as profound as they were gratuitous. For what we venerate in our gods are our own defeats *en beau.*

*

Doomed to corrupted forms of wisdom, invalids of duration, victims of time, that weakness which appalls as much as it appeals to us, we are constituted of elements that all unite to make us rebels divided between a mystic summons which has no link with history and a bloodthirsty dream which is history's symbol and nimbus. If we had a world all our own, it would matter little whether it was a world of piety or derision! We shall never have it, our position in existence lying at the intersection of our supplications and our sarcasms, a zone of impurity where sighs and provocations combine. The man too lucid to worship will also be too lucid to wreck, or will wreck only his . . . rebellions; for what is the use of rebelling only to discover, afterwards, a universe *intact?* A paltry monologue. We revolt against justice and injustice, against peace and war, against men and against the gods. Then we come around to thinking the worst old dotard may be wiser than Prometheus. Yet we do not manage to smother a scream of insurrection and continue fuming over everything and nothing: a pathetic automatism which explains why we are all statistical Lucifers.

Contaminated by the superstition of action, we believe that our ideas must *come to something.* What could be more contrary to the passive consideration of the world? But such is our fate: to be incurables who *protest*, pamphleteers on a pallet.

Our knowledge, like our experience, should paralyze us and make us indulgent to tyranny itself, once it represents a constant. We are sufficiently clear-sighted to be tempted to lay down our arms; yet the reflex of rebellion triumphs over our doubts; and though we might have made accomplished Stoics, the anarchist keeps watch within us and opposes our resignations.

"We shall never accept history": that, it seems to me, is the adage of our incapacity to be true sages, true madmen. Are we then no more than the ham-actors of wisdom and of madness? Whatever we do, with regard to our acts we are subject to a profound insincerity.

From all evidence, a believer identifies himself up to a certain point with what he does and with what he believes; there is no significant gap between his lucidity, on the one hand, and his thoughts and actions, on the other. This gap widens excessively in the *false believer*, the man who parades convictions without adhering to them. The object of his faith is a succedaneum. Bluntly: my rebellion is a faith to which I subscribe without believing in it. But I cannot *not* subscribe to it. We can never ponder enough Kirilov's description of Stavrogin: "When he believes, he doesn't believe he believes; and when he doesn't believe, he doesn't believe he doesn't believe."

*

Even more than the style, the very rhythm of our life is based on the *good standing* of rebellion. Loath to admit a universal identity, we posit individuation, heterogeneity as a primordial phenomenon. Now, to revolt is to postulate this heterogeneity, to conceive it as somehow anterior to the advent of beings and objects. If I oppose the sole truth of Unity by a necessarily deceptive Multiplicity—if, in other words, I identify the *other* with a phantom—my rebellion is meaningless, since to exist it must start from the irreducibility of individuals, from their condition as monads, circumscribed essences. Every act institutes and rehabilitates plurality, and, conferring reality and autonomy upon *the person*, implicitly recognizes the degradation, the parceling-out of *the absolute*. And it is from the act, and from the cult attached to it, that the tension of our mind proceeds, the need to explode and to destroy ourselves *at the heart of duration*. Modern philosophy, by establishing the superstition of the Ego, has made it the mainspring of our dramas and the pivot of our anxieties. To regret the repose of indistinction, the neutral dream of an existence without qualities, is pointless; we have chosen to be *subjects*, and every subject is a break with the quietude of Unity. Whoever takes it upon himself to attenuate our solitude or our lacerations acts against our interests, against our vocation. We measure an individual's value by the sum of his disagreements with things, by his incapacity to be indifferent, by his refusal as a subject to tend toward the object. Whence the obsolescence of the idea of Good; whence the vogue of the Devil.

As long as we lived amid elegant terrors, we accommodated ourselves quite well to God. When others—more sordid because more profound—took us in charge, we required another system of references, another *boss*. The Devil was the ideal figure. Everything in him agrees with the nature of the events of which he is the agent, the regulating principle: *his attributes coincide with those of time*. Let us pray to him, then, since far from being a product of our subjectivity, a creation of our need for blasphemy or solitude, he is the master of our questionings and of our panics, the instigator of our deviations. His protests, his violences have their own ambiguity: this "Great Melancholic" is a *rebel who doubts*. If he were simple, all of a piece, he would not touch us at all; but his paradoxes, his contradictions are our own: he is the sum of our impossibilities, serves as a model for our rebellions against ourselves, our self-hatred. The recipe for hell? It is in this form of revolt and hatred that it must be sought, in the torment of inverted pride, in this sensation of being a *terrible* negligible quantity, in the pangs of the "I," that "I" by which our end begins . . .

Of all fictions, that of the golden age confounds us

most: How could it have grazed our imaginations? It is in order to expose it, to denounce it, that history, *man's aggression against himself,* has taken its flight and form; so that to dedicate oneself to history is to learn to rebel, to imitate the Devil. We never imitate him so well as when, at the expense of our being, we emit time, project it outside ourselves and allow it to be converted into events. "Henceforth, time will no longer exist," announces that impromptu metaphysician who is the Angel of the Apocalypse, and thereby announces the end of the Devil, the end of history. Thus the mystics are right to seek God in themselves, or elsewhere, anywhere but in *this world* of which they make a *tabula rasa,* without for all that stooping to rebellion. They leap outside the age: a madness to which the rest of us, captives of duration, are rarely susceptible. If only we were as worthy of the Devil as they are of God!

*

To be convinced that rebellion enjoys an undue privilege among us, we need merely reflect on the manner in which we describe minds unfit for it. We call them insipid. It is virtually certain that we are closed to any form of wisdom because we see in it a transfigured insipidity. However unjust such a reaction may be, I cannot help suffering it— to Taoism itself. Even knowing that it recommends effacement and abandonment in the name of the absolute, not of cowardice, I reject it at the very moment I suppose I have adopted it; and if I acknowledge Lao Tse's victory a thousand times over, I still understand a murderer better. Between serenity and blood, it is toward blood one finds it natural to incline. Murder supposes and crowns revolt: the man who is ignorant of the desire to kill may profess all the subversive opinions he likes, he will never be anything but a conformist.

Wisdom and Revolt: two poisons. Unfit to assimilate

them naively, we find neither one a formula for salvation. The fact remains that in the Satanic adventure we have acquired a mastery we shall never possess in wisdom. For us, even *perception* is an upheaval, the beginning of a trance or an apoplexy. A loss of energy, a will to erode our available assets. Perpetual revolt involves an irreverence toward ourselves, toward our powers. How can we find in it the wherewithal for contemplation, that *static* expenditure, that concentration in immobility? To leave things as they are, to regard without trying to regulate the world, to perceive essences—nothing is more hostile to the conduct of our thought; we aspire, rather, to manipulate things, to torture them, to attribute to them our own rages. It must be so: idolators of the gesture, of the wager and of delirium, we love the daredevil, the stake-all, the desperado, as much in poetry as in philosophy. The *Tao Te Ching* goes further than *Une Saison En Enfer* or *Ecce Homo*. But Lao Tse has no delirium to propose, whereas Rimbaud and Nietzsche, acrobats straining at the extreme limits of themselves, engage us in their dangers. The only minds which seduce us are the minds which have destroyed themselves trying to give their lives a meaning.

No way out for a man who both transcends time and is bogged down in it, who accedes by fits and starts to his last solitude and nonetheless sinks into appearances. Wavering, agonized, he will drag out his days as an invalid of duration, exposed at once to the lure of becoming and of eternity. If, according to Meister Eckhart, there is an "odor" of time, there must with all the more reason be an odor of history. How can we remain insensitive to it? On a more immediate level, I distinguish the illusion, the nullity, the rottenness of "civilization"; yet I feel I belong to this rottenness: *I am the lover of carrion.* I cannot forgive our age for having subjugated us to the point of haunting us even when we detach ourselves from it. Nothing viable can emerge from a meditation on circumstances, from a reflection on the event. In other, happier times, the mind could *unreason* freely, as if it belonged to no age, emancipated as it was from the terror of chronology, engulfed in a moment of the world which it identified with the world itself. Without concern for the relativity of its work, the mind dedicated itself to that work entirely. Inspired stupidity, gone forever! Fruitful exaltation, never compromised by a consciousness drawn and quartered! Still to divine the timeless and to know nonetheless that we *are* time, that we produce time, to conceive the notion of eternity and to cherish our nothingness; an absurdity responsible for both our rebellions and the doubts we entertain about them.

To seek out suffering in order to avoid redemption, to follow in reverse the path of deliverance, such is our contribution in the matter of religion: bilious *illuminati*, Buddhas and Christs hostile to salvation, preaching to the wretched the charm of their distress. A superficial race, if you like. The fact still remains that our first ancestor left us, for our entire legacy, only the horror of paradise. By giving names to things, he prepared his own Fall and ours. And if we seek a remedy, we must begin by debaptizing the universe, by removing the label which, assigned to each appearance, isolates it and lends it a simulacrum of meaning. Meanwhile, down to our nerve cells, everything in us resists paradise. *To suffer:* sole modality of acquiring the sensation of existence; *to exist:* unique means of safeguarding our destruction. It was ever thus, and will be, as long as a cure-by-eternity has not disintoxicated us from becoming, from duration, as long as we have not approached that state in which, according to a Chinese Buddhist, "a single moment is worth ten thousand years."

*

Then since the Absolute corresponds to a meaning we have not been able to cultivate, let us surrender to all rebellions: they will end by turning against themselves, against us . . . Perhaps *then* we shall regain our supremacy over time; unless, the other way round, struggling to escape the calamity of consciousness, we rejoin animals, plants, things, return to that primordial stupidity of which, through the fault of history, we have lost even the memory.

ON A WINDED CIVILIZATION

THE MAN who belongs, organically belongs to a civilization cannot identify the nature of the disease which undermines it. His diagnosis counts for nothing; the judgment he offers upon it concerns himself; he spares the civilization out of egoism.

Less restricted, less partial, the newcomer examines it without calculation and is in a better position to grasp its failures. If it is declining, he will agree, if need be, to decline too, to remark upon it and upon himself the effects of *fatum.* As for remedies, he neither possesses nor proposes them. Since he knows you cannot *treat* destiny, he does not set himself up as a healer in any case. His sole ambition: to keep abreast of the Incurable.

*

Given the spectacle of their teeming successes, the nations of the West had no trouble exalting history, attributing to it a meaning and a finality. It belonged to them, they were its agents: hence it must take a rational course . . . Consequently they placed it under the patronage, by turns, of Providence, of Reason, and of Progress. What they lacked was a sense of fatality, which they are at last beginning to acquire, overwhelmed by the absence which lies in wait for them, by the prospect of their eclipse. Once subjects, they have become objects, forever dispossessed of that luminescence, that admirable megalomania which had hitherto protected them from the irreparable. They are so conscious of it today that they measure the stupidity of a mind by its degree of attachment to events. What is more natural, the moment events take place *elsewhere?* One reveres them only if one retains the initiative in their regard. But insofar as we cherish the memory of an old supremacy, we dream still of excelling, if only in chaos.

France, England, Germany have their age of expansion and madness behind them. Then comes *the end of insanity,* the beginning of defensive wars. No more collective crusades, no more citizens, but wan and disabused individuals, still ready to answer the call of a utopia, though on condition that it come from *somewhere else,* on condition that they need not bother to conceive it themselves. If, in the past, they died for the absurdity of glory, they abandon themselves now to a frenzy of small claims. "Happiness" tempts them; it is their last prejudice, from which Marxism, that sin of optimism, derives its energy. To blind oneself, to serve, to surrender to the ridicule or the stupidity of a cause—extravagances of which they are no longer capable. When a nation begins to show its age, it orients itself toward the condition of the masses. Even if it possessed a thousand Napoleons, it would refuse nonetheless to compromise its repose or that of the other nations. With failing reflexes, whom would it terrorize, and how? If all peoples had reached the same degree of fossilization, or of cowardice, they would readily come to an understanding: insecurity would yield to the permanence of a coward's pact . . . To

count on the disappearance of belligerent appetites, to believe in the generalization of decrepitude or in a collective
idyll is to look far ahead—too far: utopia, the presbyopia of
old nations. Young ones, scorning the lure of such vague
horizons, see matters from the viewpoint of action: their
perspective is proportionate to their enterprise. Sacrificing
comfort to adventure, happiness to efficiency, they do not
admit the legitimacy of contradictory ideas, the coexistence
of antinomic positions: their goal is to reduce our anxieties
by . . . terror, to buttress us by breaking us. All their successes derive from their savagery, since what counts, for
them, is not their dreams but their energy. If they incline to
an ideology, it is one that heightens their fury, makes the
most of their barbaric stock-in-trade, and keeps them on the
alert. When the old nations adopt one, it benumbs them,
even while affording that fractional degree of fever which
allows them to believe themselves in some sense alive: a
slight case of illusion . . .

*

A civilization exists and asserts itself only by acts of
provocation. Once it begins to calm down, it crumbles. Its
culminating moments are its formidable ones, during which,
far from husbanding its forces, it squanders them. Eager to
exhaust herself, France concentrated on wasting hers; she
succeeded, with the help of her pride, her aggressive zeal
(has she not waged, in a thousand years, more wars than any
other country?). Despite her sense of balance—even her excesses were happy ones—she could achieve supremacy only
to the detriment of her substance. To lay herself waste:
that became a point of honor. Captivated by the explosive
formula of an ideological uproar, France put her genius and
her vanity in the service of every event to occur these last
ten centuries. And, after having been a star, behold her
now—resigned, fearful, ruminating upon her regrets, her

apprehensions, and resting from her luster, from her past. She flees her countenance, trembles before the mirror . . . The wrinkles of a nation are as visible as those of an individual.

When one has made a great revolution, one does not launch another of the same importance. If one has long been the arbiter of taste, when that rank is lost, one does not try to regain it. When one craves anonymity, one is tired of serving as a model, of being followed, aped: why bother still keeping a *salon* to amuse the universe?

France knows these truisms too well to rehash them now. A nation of gestures, a theatrical nation, she loved her acting as much as her public. She is weary of it now, and wants to leave the stage. France no longer aspires to anything more than the *decors of oblivion*.

That she has used up her inspiration and her gifts we can scarcely doubt, but it would be unfair to reproach her for it: we might as well accuse her of having realized and fulfilled herself. The virtues which made her a privileged nation she has exhausted by over-civilization, by development, and it is not for lack of exercise that her talents are fading today. If the concept of *living well* (that mania of declining periods) monopolizes, obsesses her, it is because she is no more than a name for a sum of individuals, a society rather than a historic will. Her disgust for her former ambitions of universality and omnipresence has now reached such proportions that only a miracle could save her from a provincial destiny.

Ever since she abandoned her schemes for domination and conquest, France has been sapped by nostalgia, that generalized ennui. The scourge of nations on the defensive, it devastates their vitality; rather than protect themselves, they suffer it, accustom themselves to it until they can no longer do without it. Between life and death, they will always find room enough to avoid either: to escape living, to escape dying. Stricken with a lucid catalepsy, dreaming of an eternal *status quo,* how could they react against the obscurity which besets them, against the advance of opaque civilizations?

*

If we want to know what a people has been and why it is unworthy of its past, we need only examine the figures which marked it the most. What England was, the portraits of her great men show clearly enough. If you want a shock, go to the National Gallery and contemplate those virile faces, sometimes so delicate, generally monstrous—the energy they give off, the originality of their features, the arrogance and solidity of their gaze! Today's Englishmen are as remote from them as the Greeks of the Empire must have been from Aeschylus. There is nothing Elizabethan left in them: they employ what "character" they have left to save appearances. One always pays dearly for having taken "civilization" seriously, for having assimilated it *to excess.*

Who helps build an empire? Adventurers, brutes, cads—anyone without the prejudice of "man." By the end of the middle ages, England, overflowing with life, was fierce and dolorous: no concern for the *honorable thing* stood in the way of her desire for expansion. From her there emanated that melancholy of strength so characteristic of Shakespeare's characters. Hamlet's doubts fail to affect his ardor. His scruples? He provokes them by a debauch of energy, by a thirst for success, by the tension of a will *inexhaustibly* diseased: no one more liberal, more generous toward his own torments, nor so lavish with them. Luxuriant anxieties! What Englishman today could raise himself to that level? Who even tries, moreover? The English ideal for the last two hundred years has been *correct behavior,* a man *comme il faut*—an idea they have come dangerously close to realizing. The absence of vulgarity in certain circles assumes alarming dimensions: to be impersonal in England constitutes an imperative: to make others yawn becomes a law. By a pure intensity of distinction and inspidity, the

Englishman becomes more and more impenetrable and abashes us by the mystery we attribute to him in contempt of the evidence.

Reacting against his own depths, against his past behavior, undermined by prudence and reserve, he has worked up a deportment, a rule of conduct which must divide him from his own genius. Where are his exhibitions of effrontery and *hauteur*, his challenges, his old arrogances? Romanticism was the last gasp of his pride. Since then, reticent and virtuous, he has let the heritage of cynicism and insolence we thought he preened himself on crumble to dust. We should search in vain for traces of the barbarian he was: all his instincts are throttled by his decency. Instead of goading him on, encouraging his follies, his philosophers have driven him toward the impasse of happiness. Determined to be happy, he has become so. And his happiness, exempt from plenitude, from risk, from any tragic suggestion, has become that enveloping mediocrity in which he will be content forever. It is scarcely surprising he has become a character dear to the North, a model, an ideal for etiolated Vikings. As long as the Englishman was powerful, he was detested, feared; now, he is understood; soon, he will be loved . . . He is no longer a nightmare for anyone. Excess, delirium— he protects himself against these, sees them only as an aberration, or an impoliteness. What a contrast between his former excesses and the prudence he invokes now! Only at the price of great abdications does a nation become *normal*.

*

"If the sun and the moon should doubt, they'd immediately go out" (Blake). Europe has doubted for a long time . . . and if her eclipse disturbs us, the Americans and the Russians contemplate it with either composure or delight.

America stands before the world as an impetuous void, a fatality without substance. Nothing prepared her for hegemony; yet she tends toward it, not without a certain hesitation. Unlike the other nations which have had to pass through a whole series of humiliations and defeats, she has known till now only the sterility of an uninterrupted good fortune. If, in the future, everything should continue to go as well, her appearance on the scene will have been an accident without influence. Those who preside over her destiny, those who take her interests to heart, should prepare her for *bad times*; in order to cease being a superficial monster, she requires an ordeal of major scope. Perhaps she is not far from one now. Having lived, hitherto, outside hell, she is preparing to descend into it. If she seeks a destiny for herself, she will find it only on the ruins of all that was her *raison d'être*.

As for Russia, who can examine her past without feeling a thrill, a first-class *frisson*. A dim past, full of expectation, of subterranean anxiety—a past of inspired moles. The explosion of the Russians will make the nations tremble; already, they have introduced the Absolute into politics. That is the challenge they fling at a humanity gnawed by doubts and to which they will not fail to administer the *coup de grâce*. If we no longer have much soul, they have enough and to spare. Close to their origins, to that affective universe in which the mind still clings to the soil, to flesh and blood, they *feel* what they think; their truths, like their mistakes, are sensations, stimulants, acts. In fact, they do not think, they erupt. Still at the stage where the intelligence neither attenuates nor dissolves obsessions, they are as ignorant of the harmful effects of reflection as of those extremities of consciousness when it becomes the agent of uprootedness and anemia. They can therefore get under way tranquilly enough. What have they to face, except a lymphatic world? Nothing in front of them, nothing *living* with which they can collide, no obstacle: was it not a Russian who first used, in the middle of the nineteenth century, the word "cemetery" apropos of the West? Soon they will arrive *en masse* to visit the remains. Their footsteps are already perceptible

to sensitive ears. Who could oppose their advancing super-
stitions with even a simulacrum of certainty?

Since the Age of Enlightenment, Europe has ceaselessly
sapped her idols in the name of tolerance: at least, as long
as she was powerful, she believed in this idea and fought to
defend it. Even her doubts were merely convictions *disguised*; since they testified to her strength, she had the right
to speak in their name, and the means to impose them; now
they are no more than symptoms of enervation, vague impulses of an atrophied instinct.

The destruction of idols involves that of prejudices. Now,
prejudices—*organic* fictions of a civilization—assure its
duration, preserve its physiognomy. It must respect them:
if not all of them, at least those which are its own and
which, in the past, had the importance of a superstition, a
rite. If a civilization entertains them as pure conventions,
it will increasingly release itself from them without being
able to replace them by its own means. And what if it has
worshipped caprice, freedom, the individual? A high-class
conformism, no more. Once it ceases to "conform," caprice,
freedom, and the individual will become a dead letter.

A minimum of unconsciousness is necessary if one wants
to stay inside history. To act is one thing; to know one is
acting is another. When lucidity invests the action, insinuates itself into it, action is undone and, with it, prejudice,
whose function consists, precisely, in subordinating, in enslaving consciousness to action. The man who unmasks his
fictions renounces his own resources and, in a sense, himself.
Consequently, he will accept other fictions which will deny
him, since they will not have cropped up from his own
depths. No man concerned with his equilibrium may exceed
a certain degree of lucidity and analysis. How much more
this applies to a civilization, which vacillates as soon as it
exposes the errors which permitted its growth and its luster,
as soon as it calls into question *its own* truths!

One does not abuse one's capacity to doubt with impunity. When the skeptic no longer extracts any active virtue from his problems and his interrogations, he approaches his *dénouement*, indeed he seeks it out, runs to it: let others settle his uncertainties, let someone else help him to succumb! No longer knowing what to do with his anxieties, his freedom, he pines nostalgically for the executioner, even cries out for him. Those who have found answers for nothing are better at enduring the effects of tyranny than those who have found an answer for everything. Thus, when it comes to dying, dilettantes make less fuss than fanatics. During the Revolution, more than one *ci-devant* mounted the scaffold with a smile on his lips; when the Jacobins' turn came, their faces were preoccupied and somber; they were dying in the name of a truth, a prejudice. Today, wherever we look, we see only an *ersatz* truth, an *ersatz* prejudice; those who lack even this *ersatz* seem more serene, but their smile is mechanical: a poor, last reflex of elegance . . .

*

Neither the Russians nor the Americans were mature enough, nor corrupt enough intellectually to "save" Europe or to rehabilitate her decadence. The Germans, being contaminated in a different way, might have lent her a semblance of duration, a tinge of the future. But as imperialists in the name of a limited dream and of an ideology hostile to every value generated by the Renaissance, they were to accomplish their mission in reverse and spoil everything forever. Called upon to control the Continent, to give it an appearance of scope, even if only for a few generations (the twentieth century should have been German in the sense in which the eighteenth was French), they went about it so clumsily that they only hastened its downfall. Not content with having overthrown it and left it upside down, they then made a present of it to Russia and to America, for it was in *their* behalf that the Germans were good at combat and collapse. Thus, heroes on other men's account, authors of a tragic clutter, they failed in their task, their true role. After having meditated upon and elaborated the themes of the modern world, produced a Hegel, a Marx, it was their duty to apprentice themselves to a universal idea, not a tribal vision. Yet even that vision, grotesque as it was, testified in their favor: did it not reveal that they alone, in the West, preserved some vestiges of energy and barbarism, and that they were still capable of a grand design or of a vigorous insanity? But we know now that they no longer have either the desire or the capacity to hurl themselves into new adventures; that their pride, having lost its vigor, is growing as debilitated as themselves; and that, seduced in their turn by the charm of secession, they will add their modest contribution to the general collapse.

Such as it is, the West will not subsist indefinitely: it is preparing for its end, though it is in for a period of surprises . . . Think of what it was from the fifth to the tenth centuries! A much more serious crisis awaits it; another style will appear, new peoples will form. For the moment, let us envisage chaos. Already, most of us are resigned to it. Invoking History with the intention of succumbing to it, abdicating *in the name of the future*, we dream, out of a need to hope *against ourselves*, of seeing ourselves overrun, trampled down, "saved" . . . A similar sentiment had led Antiquity to that suicide which was the Christian promise.

The tired intellectual sums up the deformities and the vices of a world adrift. He does not act, he suffers; if he favors the notion of tolerance, he does not find in it the stimulant he needs. Tyranny furnishes that, as do the doctrines of which it is the outcome. If he is the first of its victims, he will not complain: only the strength that grinds him into the dust seduces him. To want to be free is to want to be oneself; but he is tired of being himself, of blazing a trail into uncertainty, of stumbling through truths. "Bind me with the chains of Illusion," he sighs, even as he says farewell to the peregrinations of Knowledge. Thus he will fling himself, eyes closed, into any mythology which will assure him the protection and the peace of the yoke. Declining the honor of assuming his own anxieties, he will engage in enterprises from which he anticipates sensations he could not derive from himself, so that the excesses of his lassitude will confirm the tyrannies. Churches, ideologies, police—seek out their origin in the horror he feels for his own lucidity, rather than in the stupidity of the masses. This weakling transforms himself, in the name of a know-nothing utopia, into a gravedigger of the intellect; convinced of doing something useful, he prostitutes Pascal's old "*abêtissez-vous*," the Solitary's tragic device.

A routed iconoclast, disillusioned with paradox and provocation, in search of impersonality and routine, half prostrated, ripe for the stereotype, the tired intellectual abdicates his singularity and rejoins the rabble. Nothing more to overturn, if not himself: the last idol to smash . . . His own debris lures him on. While he contemplates it, he shapes the idol of new gods or restores the old ones by baptizing them with new names. Unable to sustain the dignity of being fastidious, less and less inclined to winnow truths, he is content with those he is offered. By-product of his ego, he proceeds—a wrecker gone to seed—to crawl before the altars, or before what takes their place. In the temple or on the tribunal, his place is where there is singing, or shouting—no longer a chance to hear one's own voice. A parody of belief? It matters little to him, since all he aspires to is to desist from himself. All his philosophy has concluded in a refrain, all his pride foundered on a Hosanna!

Let us be fair: as things stand now, what else could he do? Europe's charm, her originality resided in the acuity of her critical spirit, in her militant, aggressive skepticism; this skepticism has had its day. Hence the intellectual, frustrated in his doubts, seeks out the compensations of dogma. Having reached the confines of analysis, struck down by the void he discovers there, he turns on his heel and attempts to seize the first certainty to come along; but he lacks the naiveté to hold onto it; henceforth, a fanatic *without convictions*, he is no more than an ideologist, a hybrid thinker, such as we find in all transitional periods. Participating in two different styles, he is, by the form of his intelligence, a tributary of the one which is vanishing, and by the ideas he defends, of the one which is appearing. To understand him better, let us imagine an Augustine half-converted, drifting and tacking, and borrowing from Christianity only its hatred of the ancient world. Are we not in a period symmetrical with the one which saw the birth of *The City of God?* It is difficult to conceive of a book more timely. Today as then, men's minds need a simple truth, an answer which delivers them from their questions, a gospel, a tomb.

The moments of refinement conceal a death-principle: nothing is more fragile than subtlety. The abuse of it leads to the catechisms, an end to dialectical games, the collapse of an intellect which instinct no longer assists. The ancient philosophy, trapped in its scruples, had in spite of itself opened the way to the artlessness of the lower depths; religious sects pullulated; the schools gave way to the cults. An analogous defeat threatens us: already the ideologies are rampant, the degraded mythologies which will reduce and annihilate us. We shall not be able to sustain the ceremony of our contradictions much longer. Many are prepared to venerate any idol, to serve any truth, so long as one and the other be imposed upon them, so long as they need not make the effort to choose their shame or their disaster.

Whatever the world to come, the Western peoples will play in it the part of the *Graeculi* in the Roman Empire. Sought out and despised by the new conqueror, they will have, in order to impress him, only the jugglery of their intelligence or the luster of their past. *The art of surviving oneself*—they are already distinguished in that. Symptoms of exhaustion are everywhere: Germany has given her measure in music: what leads us to believe that she will excel in it again? She has used up the resources of her profundity, as France those of her elegance. Both—and with them, this entire corner of the world—are on the verge of bankruptcy, the most glamorous since antiquity. Then will come the liquidation: a prospect which is not a negligible one, a respite whose duration cannot be estimated, a period of facility in which each man, before the deliverance finally at hand, will be happy to have behind him the throes of hope and expectation.

*

Amid her perplexities and inertia, Europe nonetheless preserves one conviction, only one, which she will part with for nothing in the world: the conviction that she has a future as a victim, a sacrificial future. Staunch and intractable for once, she believes herself lost, she *will be* lost, and she is. Moreover, has she not long since been taught that new races will reduce her, flout her? The moment she seemed at the pinnacle of her power, in the eighteenth century, the Abbé Galiani already observed that she was in decline and told her as much. Rousseau, for his part, prophesied: "The Tartars will become our masters: this revolution seems to me infallible." He spoke the truth. As for the next century, we know Napoleon's phrase about the Cossacks, and the prophetic agonies of a Tocqueville, a Michelet, or a Renan. These presentiments have become flesh, these intuitions now belong to the baggage of the vulgar. A man does not abdicate from one day to the next: he requires an atmosphere of retreat scrupulously maintained, a legend of defeat. This atmosphere is *created*, as is this legend. And just as the pre-Columbians, ready and resigned to suffer the invasion of distant conquerors, collapsed when the latter arrived, so the West, too learned, too conscious of its future servitude, will doubtless undertake no action in order to ward it off. It will have, moreover, neither the means nor the desire nor the audacity to do so. The crusaders, turned gardeners, vanished into that home-loving posterity in which no trace of no-madism susbsists. But history is a nostalgia for space, a horror of home, a vagabond dream and a need to die far away . . . but history is precisely what we no longer see around us.

There is a satiety which incites to discovery, to the invention of myths, of lies that instigate actions: it is an unsatisfied ardor, a morbid enthusiasm which becomes healthy as soon as it fixes upon an object; there is another kind which, dissociating the mind from its powers and life from its wellsprings, impoverishes and dessicates. Caricatured hypostasis of ennui, it destroys myths or falsifies their use. A disease, in short. To learn its symptoms and its seriousness, it would be a mistake to look far off: merely observe yourself, inspect how deeply the West has marked you . . .

*

If strength is contagious, weakness is no less so: it has its attractions, nor is it easy to resist. When the feeble are legion, they charm you, they crush you: what means is there of struggling against a continent of abulics? The disease of the will being agreeable as well, one surrenders to it with a good grace. Nothing sweeter than to drag oneself along behind events; and nothing more *reasonable*. But without a strong dose of madness, no initiative, no enterprise, no gesture. Reason: the rust of our vitality. It is the madman in us who forces us into adventure; once he abandons us, we are lost; everything depends on him, even our vegetative life; it is he who invites us, who obliges us to breathe, and it is also he who forces our blood to venture through our veins. Once he withdraws, we are alone indeed! We cannot be *normal* and *alive* at the same time. If I keep myself in a vertical position and prepare to fulfill the coming moment —if, in short, I conceive the future, a fortunate dislocation of my mind is involved. I subsist and act insofar as I am a

raving maniac, insofar as I carry my lunacies to their conclusion. Once I become reasonable, everything intimidates me:
I slide toward absence, toward springs which do not deign
to flow, toward that prostration which life must have known
before conceiving movement. I accede, *by dint of cowardice*,
to the heart of all things, clinging to an abyss I would not
dream of relinquishing, since it isolates me from becoming.
An individual, like a people, like a continent, dies out when
he shrinks from both rash plans and rash acts, when, instead
of taking risks and hurling himself toward being, he cowers
within it, takes refuge there: a metaphysics of regression, a
retreat to the primordial! In her terrible equilibrium, Europe
rejects herself, along with the memory of her impertinences
and her bravados, and even her *passion for the inevitable*,
the last honor of defeat. Refractory to every form of excess,
to every form of life, she deliberates, she will always deliberate, even after she has ceased to exist: does she not already
produce the effect of a council of spectres?

. . . I remember a poor wretch who, still in bed at noon,
addressed himself in imperative tones: "Will! Will!" The
farce was repeated every day: he was imposing upon himself
a task he could not accomplish. At least, acting against the
ghost he was, he scorned the delights of his own lethargy.
One cannot say as much for Europe. Having discovered, at
the end of her efforts, the realm of non-will, she rejoices, for
she knows now that her ruin conceals a pleasure principle,
and she intends to profit by it. Abandonment enchants and
fulfills her. Time continues to pass? She is not at all
alarmed; let others bother about time; it is their business:
they do not guess what relief there can be in wallowing in a
present that leads nowhere . . .

To live here is death; elsewhere, suicide. Where can one
go? The only part of the planet where existence seemed to
have some justification is tainted with gangrene. These
arch-civilized peoples are our purveyors of despair. To de-

spair, as a matter of fact, it suffices to look at them, to observe the machinations of their minds and the indigence of
their dampened, nearly extinguished lusts. After having
sinned so long against their origin and neglected the savage,
the horde—their point of departure—they are forced to
realize they no longer possess a single drop of Hun blood.

The ancient historian who remarked of Rome that she
could no longer endure either her vices nor their remedies
did not so much define his own epoch as anticipate ours.
Great was the Empire's lassitude, no doubt, but it was
still chaotic and inventive enough to put its enemies off
the scent, to cultivate cynicism, ceremony, and ferocity,
whereas the Empire we are watching now possesses. in its
rigorous mediocrity, none of the prestige which produces
. . . illusion. Too flagrant, too explicit, it suggests a disease
whose ineluctable automatism might reassure, paradoxically,
both patient and practitioner: an agony in good and due
form, precise as a contract, a stipulated agony, without
whims or lacerations, made to the measure of peoples who,
not content with having rejected the prejudices which stimulate life, reject into the bargain the one which justifies and
establishes it: the prejudice of becoming.

A collective entry into vacuity! But let us make no mistake about it: this vacuity, different at every point from
the kind Buddhism calls the "seat of truth," is neither fulfillment nor liberation; not positive experience expressed in
negative terms, not the effort of meditation, a will to *askesis*
and nakedness, a conquest of salvation; rather a capitulation,
a decline without nobility and without passion. Product of
an anemic metaphysic, it cannot be the recompense of experiment, the reward of sacrifice. The Orient advances
toward a Void of its own, expands in it, and triumphs there,
while we bog down in ours and lose our last resources.
Decidedly, everything is degraded and corrupted in our consciousness: even the Void is impure.

So many conquests, acquisitions, ideas—where w'll they find their continuation? In Russia? In North America? Each has already drawn the consequences of the worst of Europe . . . Latin America? South Africa? Australia? It is from this direction that we must, it appears, expect our relief, the changing of the guard.

The future belongs to the suburbs of the globe.

A LITTLE THEORY OF DESTINY

CERTAIN peoples—the Russians, for example, and the Spanish—are so haunted by themselves that they *pose themselves* as a unique problem: their development, singular at every point, compels them to fall back on their series of anomalies, on the miracle or the insignificance of their fate.

Russia's literary beginnings were, in the last century, a kind of apogee, a lightninglike success which inevitably disturbed her: it was only natural that she should be a surprise to herself and that she should exaggerate her importance. Dostoevsky's characters put Russia on the same footing as God, since they extend to the former the mode of interrogation applied to the latter: must we believe in Russia? Must we deny her? Does she really exist, or is she nothing but an excuse? To question oneself in this fashion is to pose a regional problem in theological terms. But for Dostoevsky, as a matter of fact, Russia, far from being a regional problem, was a universal one, to the same degree as the existence of God. Such an approach, abusive and preposterous, was possible only in a country whose abnormal evolution must astound or confound men's minds. It is hard to imagine an

Englishman wondering if England has a meaning or not, or assigning her, with tremendous rhetoric, a mission: he knows he is English, and that is sufficient. The evolution of his country does not entail an essential interrogation.

Among the Russians, messianism derives from an inner uncertainty, aggravated by pride, from a determination to assert their faults, to impose them on others, to discharge a suspect overflow upon them. The aspiration to "save" the world is the morbid phenomenon of a people's youth.

*

Spain is self-absorbed for the contrary reasons. She, too, had dazzling beginnings, but they are faraway now. Having arrived too soon, she convulsed the world, then allowed herself to decline and fall: and one day, I had a revelation of that fall. It was in Valladolid, in the Casa Cervantes. An ordinary-looking old woman was standing next to me, looking at the portrait of Philip III: "A madman," I said. She turned toward me: "It was with him that our decadence began." I was at the heart of the problem. "Our decadence!" There we have it, I thought, in Spain decadence is a popular concept, a national cliché, an official slogan. The nation which in the sixteenth century offered the world a spectacle of magnificence and madness—is now reduced to codifying her inertia. If they had had time for it, doubtless the last Romans would not have proceeded otherwise; but they were unable to ponder their fall, for the Barbarians already surrounded them. Better provided for, the Spanish have had the leisure (three centuries!) to meditate on their miseries, to saturate themselves in them. Gossips of despair, improvisers of illusions, they live in a kind of melodious asperity, a *tragic non-seriousness*, which saves them from vulgarity, from happiness and from success. Should they someday exchange their ancient fads for other, more modern ones, they would nonetheless remain marked by so long an absence. Incapable of falling into step with "civilization," bigots or anarchists, they could never renounce their *inactuality*. How could they overtake the other nations, how could they be up to date, when they have exhausted the best of themselves ruminating on death, befouling themselves with it, turning it into a visceral experience? Constantly retrogressing toward the essential, they have capsized out of their depths—i.e., in them. The notion of decadence would not preoccupy them so much if it did not translate in terms of history their weakness for the void, their obsession with the skeleton. Nothing surprising in the fact that for each of them, his country should be *his* problem. Reading Ganivet, Unamuno, or Ortega, we realize that for them Spain is a paradox which touches them intimately and which they cannot reduce to a rational formula. They return to it constantly, fascinated by the attraction of the insoluble which it represents. Unable to solve it by analysis, they contemplate Don Quixote, in whom the paradox is even more insoluble, being a symbol . . . We do not imagine a Valéry or a Proust meditating on France in order to discover themselves: a country intact, without the deep rifts that breed anxiety, a non-tragic nation, France is not a case: having succeeded, having concluded her fate, how could she be "interesting"?

It is the merit of Spain to propose a type of unwonted development, a destiny both inspired and incomplete. (One might say, a Rimbaud incarnated in a collectivity.) Think of Spain's frenzied pursuit of gold, her collapse into anonymity, then think of the conquistadors, their banditry and their piety, the way they associated the Gospels with murder, the Crucifix with the sword. At its finest moments, Catholicism was sanguinary, as is proper for any truly inspired religion.

Conquest and Inquisition—parallel phenomena, products of Spain's imposing vices. As long as she was strong, she excelled in massacres, and to them brought not only her partiality for ceremony, but also the innermost realms of her sensibility. Only cruel peoples have the chance to approach the very sources of life, its palpitations, its kindling arcana: life reveals its essence only to eyes inflamed with blood-lust . . . How can we believe in philosophies when we know what pale faces they reflect? The habit of reasoning, of speculation, is the sign of a vital inadequacy, a decline in affectivity. To think methodically, a man must, with the help of his deficiencies, forget himself, no longer be an integral part of his ideas: philosophy, the privilege of individuals and of *biologically* superficial peoples.

It is almost impossible to talk to a Spaniard about anything but his country, a closed universe that is the subject of his lyricism and his reflections, an absolute province, outside the world. Alternately exalted and downcast, he turns his morose and dazzled eyes upon Spain; being drawn and quartered is his form of rigor. If he allows himself a future, he does not really believe in it. His discovery: the somber illusion, the pride of despair; his genius: the genius of nostalgia.

Whatever his political orientation, the Spaniard or the Russian who questions himself about his country treats the only question that matters in his eyes. We understand why neither Spain nor Russia has produced a major philosopher. It is because the philosopher must attack ideas as a spectator; before assimilating them, making them his own, he must consider them from outside, dissociate himself from them, weigh them, and, if need be, *play* with them; then, with the help of maturity, he elaborates a system with which he never altogether identifies himself. It is this superiority with regard to their own philosophy we admire in the Greeks. The same is true for all those who attach themselves to the problem of knowledge and make it the essential object of their meditation. This problem troubles neither the Russians nor the Spanish. Unsuited to intellectual contemplation, they maintain quite bizarre relations with the Idea. If they challenge it, they always have the *under hand*; it seizes, subjugates, oppresses them; consenting martyrs, they ask only to suffer for it. With them, we are far from the domain where the mind plays with itself and with things, far from any methodical perplexity.

The abnormal evolution of Russia and Spain has therefore led them to question themselves as to their own destiny. But these are two great nations, despite their lacunae and their accidents of growth. For the minor peoples, how much more tragic the national problem becomes! No sudden expansion here, no gradual decadence either. Without a prop in the future or in the past, they weigh upon *themselves*: a long sterile meditation is the result. Their evolution cannot be abnormal, for they do not evolve. What is left to them? Resignation to themselves, since, outside, there is all of History from which, precisely, they are excluded.

Their nationalism, which we take for a farce, is actually a mask by which they try to hide their own drama and to forget, in a frenzy of claims, their incapacity to graft themselves onto events: painful lies, an exasperated reaction against the scorn they fear to deserve, a way of conjuring away their secret obsession with themselves. In simpler terms: a people which is a torment to itself is a sick people. But whereas Spain suffers for having exited from History, and Russia for seeking, in spite of all opposition, to install herself there, the minor nations struggle in order to have none of these reasons to lose patience or to despair. Cursed with an original flaw, they cannot remedy it by disappointment, or by dreams. Hence they have no other resources than to be haunted by themselves. An obsession not lacking in beauty, since it leads to nothing and interests no one.

*

There are countries which enjoy a kind of benediction, a kind of grace: everything succeeds for them, even their misfortunes, even their catastrophes; and there are others which cannot carry it off, whose very triumphs are equivalent to failures. When they seek to assert themselves, to leap forward, an external fatality intervenes to break their spring and bring them back to their point of departure. All occasions are taken from them, even that of ridicule.

To be French is obvious enough: one neither suffers from it, nor does one rejoice over it; one possesses a certainty which justifies the old interrogation: "How can one be a Persian?"

The paradox of being a Persian (or as the case would have it, a Rumanian) is a torment one must know how to exploit, a defect by which one must profit. I confess I once regarded it as a disgrace to belong to an ordinary nation, to a collectivity of victims about whose origin no illusion was permitted. I believed, and I was perhaps not mistaken, that we had sprung from the lees of the Barbarians, from the scum of the great Invasions, from those hordes which, unable to pursue their march West, collapsed along the Carpathians and the Danube, somnolently squatting there, a mass of deserters on the Empire's confines, daubed with a touch of Latinity. With that past, this present. And this future. What an ordeal for my young arrogance! "How can one be a Rumanian?" was a question I could answer only by a constant mortification. Hating my people, my country, its timeless peasants enamored of their own torpor and almost bursting with hebetude, I blushed to be descended from them, repudiated them, rejected their sub-eternity, their larval certainties, their geologic reverie. No use scanning their features for the fidgets, the grimaces of revolt: the monkey, alas! was dying in them. In truth, did they not sprout from the very rock? Unable to rouse them, or to animate them, I came to the point of dreaming of an extermination. One does not massacre stones. The spectacle they offered me justified and baffled, nourished and disgusted my hysteria. And I never stopped cursing the accident that caused me to be born among them.

One great idea possessed them: the idea of destiny. I repudiated it with all my strength, saw in it nothing but the subterfuge of poltroons, an excuse for every abdication, an expression of common sense and its funereal philosophy. What could I cling to? My country whose existence, obviously, made no sense seemed to me a résumé of nothingness or a materialization of the inconceivable, a sort of Spain without its *Siglo de Oro*, without conquests or madness, and without a Don Quixote of our woes. To belong to it—what a lesson in humiliation and sarcasm, what a calamity, what a leprosy!

As for the great idea that prevailed there, I was too impertinent, too conceited to perceive its origin, its depth, or its experiences, the system of disasters which it supposed. I was not to understand it until much later. How it finally insinuated itself, I do not know. When I was led to experience it lucidly, I became reconciled to my country which, *thereupon*, at last ceased to haunt me.

To exempt themselves from action, oppressed peoples entrust themselves to "fate," a negative salvation as well as a means of interpreting events: a philosophy of history *for daily use*, a determinist vision on an effective basis, a metaphysic of circumstance . . .

If the Germans, too, are sensitive to destiny, they see it, nonetheless, not as a principle intervening from outside, but as a force which, emanating from their will, ends by escaping them and turning against them in order to crush them. Linked to their appetite for demiurgic power, their *Schicksal* supposes a play of fatalities not so much within the world as within the self. Which comes down to saying that up to a certain point it depends on them.

To conceive destiny as exterior to ourselves, omnipotent and sovereign, a vast cycle of failures is requisite. A condition which my country fulfills to perfection. It would be indecent for Rumania to believe in effort, in the utility of action. Hence it does not believe in them and, out of propriety, resigns itself to the inevitable. I am grateful to it for having bequeathed me, with the code of despair, that *savoir-*

vivre, that relaxation in the face of Necessity, as well as several impasses and the art of adjusting to them. Prompt to sustain my disappointments and to initiate my indolence into the secret of preserving them, my country has further offered me, in its eagerness to make me into a wastrel who keeps up appearances, the means of degrading myself without compromising myself too much. I owe it not only my finest, my surest failures, but also this talent for masking my cowardice and hoarding my compunctions. For how many other advantages am I not in its debt! Its titles to my gratitude are so numerous, in fact, that it would be boring to list them here.

Whatever good will I might have mustered, would I have been able, without my country, to waste my days in so exemplary a manner? It has helped me to do so, led me on, encouraged me. To spoil one's life, one forgets all too quickly, is not so easy: it takes a tradition, long training, the labor of several generations. This labor performed, everything goes perfectly. The certainty of Futility then forms part of your inheritance: it is a possession your ancestors have acquired for you by the sweat of their brow and at the cost of countless humiliations. As for your own humiliations, you will always be able to embellish or evade them, to affect the manner of an elegant no-good, to be, honorably, the last among men. Politeness, the urbanity of misfortune, privilege of those who, born failures, have begun by their end. To know oneself of a breed which has never been is a bitterness alloyed with a certain sweetness, even a certain voluptuousness.

The exasperation I used to feel when I heard anyone say, apropos of one thing or another: "it's fate," now seems childish to me. I didn't realize then that I would come to do as much; that, taking shelter behind this syllable myself, I would ascribe to it good luck and bad, all the details of happiness and disaster; that, further, I would cling to Destiny with the ecstasy of a shipwrecked mariner, would address my first thoughts to it before flinging myself into the horror of each day. "You will vanish into space, O my Russia," Tyuchev exclaimed in the last century. I applied his exclamation with more suitability to my own country, much better constituted in order to be engulfed, provided with all the qualities of an ideal and anonymous victim. The habit of endless and pointless suffering, the plenitude of disaster—what an apprenticeship in the school of vanquished tribes! This is how the oldest Rumanian historian begins his chronicles: "It is not man who commands the times, but the times which command man." A crude formula, program and epitaph of one corner of Europe. To catch the tone of Balkan popular sensibility, one need only recall the lamentations of the chorus in Greek tragedy. By an unconscious tradition, a whole ethnic space was marked by it. Routine of the sigh and of calamity, jeremiads of minor peoples before the bestiality of the great! Yet let us be careful not to complain too much: is it not comforting to oppose to the world's disorders the coherence of our miseries and our defeats? And have we not, in the face of universal dilettantism, the consolation of possessing, with regard to pain, a professional competence?

ADVANTAGES OF EXILE

IT IS A mistake to think of the expatriate as someone who abdicates, who withdraws and humbles himself, resigned to his miseries, his outcast state. On a closer look, he turns out to be ambitious, aggressive in his disappointments, his very acrimony qualified by his belligerence. The more we are dispossessed, the more intense our appetites and our illusions become. I even discern some relation betwen misfortune and megalomania. The man who has lost everything preserves as a last resort the hope of glory, or of literary scandal. He consents to abandon everything, except his *name*. But how will he impose his name when he writes in a language of which the cultivated are either ignorant or contemptuous?

Will he venture into another idiom? It will not be easy for him to renounce the words on which his past hinges. A man who repudiates his language for another changes his identity, even his disappointments. Heroic apostate, he breaks with his memories and, to a certain point, with himself.

*

Let us say a man writes a novel which makes him, over-night, a celebrity. In it he recounts his sufferings. His compatriots in exile envy him: they too have suffered, perhaps more. And the man without a country becomes—or aspires to become—a novelist. The consequence: an accumulation of confusions, an inflation of horrors, of *frissons* that *date*. One cannot keep renewing Hell, whose very characteristic is monotony, or the face of Exile either. Nothing in literature exasperates a reader so much as The Terrible; in life, it is too tainted with the obvious to rouse our interest. But our author persists; for the time being he buries his novel in a drawer and awaits his hour. The illusion of a surprise, of a renown which eludes his grasp but on which he reckons, sustains him; he lives on unreality. Such, however, is the power of this illusion that if, for instance, he works in some factory, it is with the notion of being freed from it one day or another by a fame as sudden as it is inconceivable.

*

Equally tragic is the case of the poet. Walled up in his own language, he writes for his friends—for ten, for twenty persons at the most. His longing to be read is no less imperious than that of the improvised novelist. At least he has the advantage over the latter of being able to get his verses published in the little *émigré* reviews which appear at the cost of almost indecent sacrifices and renunciations. Let us say such a man becomes—transforms himself—into an editor of such a review; to keep his publication alive he risks hunger, abstains from women, buries himself in a window-less room, imposes privations which confound and appall. Tuberculosis and masturbation, that is his fate.

No matter how scanty the number of *émigrés*, they form groups, not to protect their interests but to get up subscriptions, to bleed each other white in order to publish their regrets, their cries, their echoless appeals. One cannot conceive of a more heart-rending form of the gratuitous.

That they are as good poets as they are bad prose-writers is to be accounted for readily enough. Consider the literary production of any "minor" nation which has not been so childish as to make up a past for itself: the abundance of poetry is its most striking characteristic. Prose requires, for its development, a certain rigor, a differentiated social status, and a tradition: it is deliberate, constructed; poetry *wells up*: it is direct or else totally fabricated; the prerogative of cave men or aesthetes, it flourishes only on the near or far side of civilization, never at the center. Whereas prose demands a premeditated genius and a crystallized language, poetry is perfectly compatible with a barbarous genius and a formless language. To create a *literature* is to create a prose.

*

What could be more natural than that so many possess no other mode of expression than poetry? Even those who are not particularly gifted draw, in their uprooted state, upon the automatism of their exclusion, that bonus talent they would never have found in a normal existence.

In whatever form it happens to take, and whatever its cause, exile—at its start—is an academy of intoxication. And it is not given to everyone to be intoxicated. It is a limit-situation and resembles the extremity of the poetic state. Is it not a *favor* to be transported to that state straight off, without the detours of a discipline, by no more than the benevolence of fatality? Think of Rilke, that expatriate *de luxe*, and of the number of solitudes he had to accumulate in order to liquidate his connections, in order to establish a foothold in the invisible. It is not easy to be *nowhere*, when no external condition obliges you to do so. Even the mystic attains his *askesis* only at the cost of monstrous efforts. To extricate oneself from the world—what a labor of abolition! The exile achieves it without turning a hair, by the cooperation—i.e., the hostility—of history. No torments, no vigils in order for him to strip himself of everything; events compel him. In a sense, he is like the invalid who also installs himself in metaphysics or in poetry without personal merit, by the force of circumstances, by the good offices of disease. A trumpery absolute? Perhaps, though it is not proved that the results acquired by effort exceed in value those which derive from a surrender to the inescapable.

*

One danger threatens the exiled poet: that of adapting himself to his fate, of no longer suffering from it, of enjoying himself because of it. No one can keep his griefs in their prime; they use themselves up. The same is true of homesickness, of any nostalgia. Regrets lose their luster, wear themselves out by their own momentum, and after the fashion of the elegy, quickly fall into desuetude. What then is more natural than to establish oneself in exile, the Nowhere City, a *patrie* in reverse? To the degree that he revels in it, the poet erodes the substance of his emotions, the resources of his misery as well as his dreams of glory. The curse from which he drew pride and profit no longer afflicting him, he loses, along with it, both the energy of his exceptional status and the reasons for his solitude. Rejected by Hell, he will try in vain to reinstate himself there, to be reinvigorated by it: his sufferings, too mild now, will make him forever unworthy of it. The cries of which he was only yesterday still proud have become bitterness, and bitterness does not become verse: it will lead him beyond poetry. No more songs, no more excesses. His wounds healed, there is no use pointing to them in order to extract certain accents: at best he will be the epigone of his pains. An honorable downfall awaits him. Lacking diversity, original anxieties, his inspiration dries up. Soon, resigned to anonymity and even intrigued by his mediocrity, he will assume the mask of a bourgeois from *nowhere in particular*. Thus he reaches the end of his lyrical career, the most stable point of his degeneration.

*

"Fixed up," established in the comfort of his fall, what will he do next? He will have the choice between two forms of salvation: faith and humor. If he drags along some vestiges of anxiety, he will gradually liquidate them by means of a thousand prayers; unless he consoles himself with a reassuring metaphysic, pastime of exhausted versifiers. And if, on the contrary, he is inclined to mockery, he will minimize his defeats to the point of rejoicing in them. According to his temperament, he will therefore sacrifice to piety or to sarcasm. In either case, he will have triumphed over his ambitions, as over his misfortunes, in order to achieve a higher goal, in order to become a decent victim, a respectable outcast.

A PEOPLE OF
SOLITARIES

I SHALL attempt to extemporize upon the ordeals of a people, upon its history which baffles History, upon its fate which seems to derive from a supernatural logic, in which the unheard-of mingles with the obvious, miracle with necessity. Some call it a race, some a nation, others a tribe. Since it resists classification, whatever precise things we can say will be inexact; no definition is quite applicable. To apprehend it best, we must resort to some special category, for here everything is unfamiliar: Is this people not the first to have colonized heaven, to have placed *its* God there? As impatient to create myths as to destroy them, it has forged for itself a religion on which it prides itself, of which it is ashamed . . . For all its lucidity, this people readily sacrifices to illusion: it hopes, it always hopes too much . . . A strange conjunction of energy and analysis, of irony and thirst. With so many enemies, any other people, in its place, would have laid down its arms; but this nation, unsuited to the complacencies of despair, bypassing its age-old fatigue and the conclusions imposed by its fate, lives in the delirium of expectation, determined not to learn a lesson from its humiliations, nor to deduce from them a rule of diffidence, a principle of anonymity. It prefigures the universal diaspora: its past summarizes our future. The more closely we scrutinize our tomorrows, the closer we come to and the more we flee this people: all of us tremble at the obligation to resemble it some day . . . "Soon you will be following in my footsteps," this nation seems to tell us, even as it draws, above our certainties, a question mark.

*

To be a man is a drama; to be a Jew is another. Hence the Jew has the privilege of living our condition *twice over*. He represents the alienated existence *par excellence* or, to utilize an expression by which the theologians describe God, the *wholly other*. Conscious of his singularity, he thinks of it constantly and never forgets himself; whence that constrained, tense, or falsely assured expression, so frequent in those who bear the burden of a secret. Instead of priding himself on his origins, of advertising and declaring them, he camouflages them: yet does not his unique fate confer upon him the right to regard the human rabble with disdain? A victim, he reacts in his own way, a loser *sui generis*. In more than one way, he is related to that serpent out of which he made a character and a symbol. Yet we shall not suppose that he, too, is cold-blooded: that would be to ignore his true nature, his enthusiasms, his capacity for love and hate, his thirst for vengeance or the eccentricities of his charity. (Certain Hassidic rabbis yield nothing in this matter to the Christian saints.) Excessive in everything, emancipated from the tyranny of local commitment, from the stupidities of *enracinement*, without attachments, acosmic, he is the man who will never be *from here*, the man from somewhere else, the stranger *as such* who cannot unambiguously speak in the name of the natives, of *all*. To translate their feelings, to make himself their interpreter—what a task, should he lay claim to it! There is no crowd he can lead on, sweep

away, arouse: the trumpet is not his *forte*. He will be reproached for his parents, his ancestors who lie at rest far
away, in other countries, other continents. Without graves
to point to, to exploit, without means of being the spokes-
man of any cemetery, he represents no one, if not himself.
Does he originate the latest slogan? Does he stand at the
source of a revolution? He will find himself cast out at the
very moment his ideas triumph, when his words have the
force of law. If he makes use of a cause, he cannot take advantage of it to the end. A day comes when he must contemplate it as a spectator, and a disappointed one at that.
Then he will defend another cause, with no less ringing
rebuffs. If he changes his country, his drama merely begins
again: exodus is his seat, his certainty, his *chez soi*.

*

Better and worse than us, he embodies the extremes to
which we aspire without achieving them: he is *us* when we
are beyond ourselves . . . Since his holdings in the absolute
exceed our own, he offers—in good, in evil—the ideal image
of our capacities. His comfort in imbalance, the routine he
has acquired there, make him a nervous wreck, an expert in
psychiatry as in every kind of therapeutics, a theoretician of
his own diseases: he is not, like us, abnormal by accident or
out of snobbery, but naturally, without effort, and by tradition: such is the advantage of an inspired destiny on the
scale of a whole people. An anxiety-victim oriented toward
action, a sick man unsuited to repose, he nurses himself on
the move and *moving forward*. His reverses do not resemble
ours: even in disaster he rejects conformity. His history—
an interminable schism.

*

Persecuted in the name of the Lamb, doubtless he will
remain non-Christian as long as Christianity is in power.
But so greatly does he love paradox—and the sufferings that

result from it—that he will perhaps convert to the Christian religion at the moment it is universally reviled. He will then be persecuted for his new faith. Possessed of a religious destiny, he has survived Athens and Rome, as he will survive the West, and he will pursue his career, envied and despised by all peoples that are born and die . . .

*

When the churches are deserted forever, the Jews will return to them, or will build others, or, what is more likely, will plant the Cross on the synagogues. Meanwhile, they wait for Jesus to be abandoned: will they see in him then their true messiah? We shall find out at the end of the Church . . . , for unless there is some unforeseeable degradation, they will not deign to kneel beside Christians, or to gesticulate with them. They would have acknowledged Christ if he had not been accepted by the nations and had he not become a common property, an export messiah. Under the Roman domination, they were the only ones not to allow the statues of the emperors in their temples; forced to do so, they rebelled. Their messianic hope was less a dream of conquering other nations than of destroying their gods for the glory of Jahweh: sinister theocracy, that opposed polytheism with its skeptical tonalities. Since they kept apart within the empire, they were accused of crime, for their exclusivism was not understood, nor their refusal to sit down to table with strangers, to participate in games, in spectacles, to mingle with others and respect their customs. They credited only their own prejudices, whence the accusation of "misanthropy," a crime imputed to them by Cicero, Seneca, Celsius, and, with them, all antiquity. As early as 130 B.C., during the siege of Jerusalem by Antiochus, the latter's friends advised him to "seize the city by main force, and to annihilate completely the Jewish race; for alone of all nations, it refused all social bonds with other peoples, and considered them as enemies" (Poseidonios of Apamea). Did they relish their role as undesirables? Did they seek to be alone on earth in principle? Certainly they appeared for a long time as the very incarnation of fanaticism, and their inclination for liberal ideas is rather acquired than innate. The most intolerant and the most persecuted of peoples unites universalism with the strictest particularism. A natural contradiction: futile attempting to resolve or to explain it.

Worn threadbare, Christianity has ceased to be a source of scandal and surprise, to precipitate crises or to fertilize intelligences. It no longer inconveniences the mind nor enforces the least interrogation; the anxieties it provokes, like its answers and its solutions, are flabby, soporific: no fruitful self-torment, no drama can start here. It has served its term: already we yawn over the Cross . . . To attempt to save Christianity, to prolong its career, would not occur to us; on occasion it awakens our . . . indifference. After having occupied our depths, it barely manages to sustain itself on our surface; soon, supplanted, it will be added to the total of our unsuccessful experiments. Consider the cathedrals: having lost the impulse that supported their mass, turned back into *stone*, they shrink and slip; their very steeples, which once pointed insolently to heaven, suffer the contamination of weight and imitate the modesty of our lassitudes.

When we happen to make our way inside one of them we think of the futility of the prayers offered, of so many fevers and follies wasted . . . Soon the void will reign here. Nothing gothic is left in the substance, nothing gothic left in ourselves. If Christianity preserves a semblance of reputation, it is due to the backward who, pursuing it with a retrospective hatred, would pulverize the two thousand years in which, by some wile, it has obtained the acquiescence of men's minds. Since these retarded creatures, these haters, are becoming increasingly rare, and since Christianity finds no comfort for the loss of so lasting a popularity, it seeks on all sides an event likely to restore it to the foreground, to actuality. To become "curious" once again, Christianity would have to be raised to the dignity of an accursed sect; only the Jews could take it over: they would project enough strangeness into it to renew it, to rejuvenate its mystery. Had they adopted it at the right moment, they would have suffered the fate of so many other peoples whose name history barely preserves. It was to spare themselves such a fate that they rejected it. Leaving to the Gentiles the ephemeral advantages of salvation, they opted for the lasting disadvantages of perdition. Infidelity? That is the censure which, after Saint Paul, continues to pursue them. A ridiculous criticism, since their fault consists precisely of an excessive loyalty to themselves. Beside them, the first Christians look like opportunists: sure of their cause, they cheerfully awaited martyrdom. By exposing themselves to it, they did no more than sacrifice to the *mores* of a period when the taste for spectacular blood-lettings made the sublime an easy matter.

Quite different is the case of the Jews. By refusing to follow the ideas of the times, the great madness which had seized the world, they provisionally escaped persecution. But at what cost! For not having shared the momentary ordeals of the new fanatics, they were subsequently to bear the burden and the terror of the Cross; indeed it was for them, and not for the Christians, that it became the symbol of torture.

Throughout the Middle Ages, they were massacred because they had crucified one of their own . . . No people has paid so dearly for a rash but explicable and, all things considered, natural gesture. At least so it seemed to me when I witnessed the "Passion Play" at Oberammergau. In the conflict between Jesus and the authorities, it was, of course, with Jesus that the public sided, amid copious tears. Struggling in vain to do as much, I felt quite *alone* in that audience. What had happened? I found myself at a trial in which the prosecution's arguments struck me by their accuracy. Annas and Caiaphas embodied, to my eyes, good sense itself. Employing honest methods, they showed remarkable interest in the case before them. Perhaps they asked for nothing better than to be converted. I shared their exasperation over the evasive answers of the accused. Irreproachable on every point, they used no theological or juridical subterfuge: a perfect interrogation. Their probity won me over: I sided with them and approved of Judas, though scorning his remorse. From that point on, the *dénouement* of the conflict left me indifferent. And when I walked out of the hall, I felt that the public was perpetuating by its tears a misunderstanding two thousand years old.

However grave its consequences may have been, the rejection of Christianity remains the Jews' finest exploit, a *no* which does them honor. If previously they had walked alone by necessity, they would henceforth do so by resolve, as outcasts armed with a great cynicism, the sole precaution they have taken against their future . . .

*

Imbued with their fits of conscience, the Christians, gratified that another should have suffered for them, loll in the shadow of Calvary. If they sometimes busy themselves retracing its stages, what advantage they manage to derive from doing so! With the look of profiteers, they *bloom* in church and, when they leave, scarcely dissimulate that smile produced by a certitude gained without fatigue. Grace, of course, is on their side, a bargain Grace and a suspect one which spares them from making any effort. Carnival "redeemed," braggarts of redemption, sensualists caressed by humility, sin, and hellfire: if they torment their conscience, it is to procure themselves sensations. They procure others by tormenting yours. Once they detect scruple, division or the obsessive presence of a sin or a transgression, they will never let you go, but oblige you to exhibit your agony or advertise your guilt, while they watch like Sadists the spectacle of your confusion. Weep if you can: that is what they are waiting for, impatient to get drunk on your tears, to wallow, charitable and grim, in your himiliations, to feast on your griefs. These men of conviction are so greedy for suspect sensations that they seek them everywhere, and when they no longer find any in the world outside, rush upon themselves. Far from being haunted by the truth, the Christian marvels at his "inner conflicts," at his vices and his virtues, at their power of intoxication, gloats over the Cross and, an Epicurean of the horrible, associates pleasure with sentiments which generally involve nothing of the kind: has he not invented the *orgasm* of repentance?

Although *chosen*, the Jews were to gain no advantage by that privilege: neither peace nor salvation . . . Quite the contrary, it was imposed upon them as an ordeal, as a punishment. *A chosen people without Grace.* Thus their prayers have all the more merit in that they are addressed to a God without an alibi.

Not that the Gentiles are to be condemned *en masse.* But they haven't much of which to be so proud: they calmly belong to the "human race" . . . Which is what, from Nebuchadnezzar to Hitler, they have not been willing to allow the Jews; unfortunately, the latter have not had the courage to pride themselves on this. With an arrogance of the gods, they should have boasted their differences, proclaimed in the face of the universe that they had no like on earth nor sought to have, should have spat on races and empires and, in a burst of self-destruction, should have supported the theses of their detractors, should have sustained those who hate them . . . Let us leave aside regrets, or delirium. Who dares take upon himself the arguments of his enemies? Such an order of greatness, scarcely conceivable in an individual, is not to be entertained on the level of a people. The instinct of self-preservation mars individuals and collectivities alike.

If the Jews had to face only the professional antisemite, their drama would thereby be singularly diminished. At grips, however, with the quasi-totality of humanity, they know that antisemitism does not represent a phenomenon of one period or another, but a constant, and that yesterday's exterminators used the same terms as Tacitus . . . The inhabitants of the globe are divided into two categories: Jews and non-Jews. If we were to weigh the merits of the former and the latter, uncontestably the former would prevail; they would have sufficient qualification to speak in the name of humanity, and to consider themselves its representatives. They will not find it in their hearts to do so as long as they preserve some respect, some weakness for the rest of the human race. What an idea, to want to be loved! They impose it upon themselves without success. After so many fruitless attempts, would they not be better off yielding to the obvious, admitting at last the substantiation of their disappointments?

*

No events, no crimes or catastrophes for which their adversaries have not made them responsible. Extravagant homage. Not that we need minimize their role; but to be just, we must consider only their real misdeeds: the chief of which remains that of having produced a God Whose fortunes— unique in the history of religions—may well leave us something to think about; nothing about Him justifies such a success: bickering, crude, capricious, verbose, He could at best correspond to the necessities of a tribe; that one day He should become the object of learned theologies, the patron of highly developed civilizations, no one could have foreseen, certainly. If the Jews have not inflicted Him upon us, they nevertheless bear the responsibility of having conceived Him. That is a flaw in their genius. They could have done better. However vigorous, however virile He may seem, their Jahweh (of which Christianity offers us a revised version) infallibly inspires in us a certain mistrust. Instead of getting flustered, seeking to impose Himself, He should have been, given his functions, more correct, more distinguished, and above all more assured. Uncertainties trouble Him: He shrieks, storms, fulminates . . . Is that a sign of power? For all His grand airs, we discern the apprehensions of a usurper who, sensing danger, fears for his kingdom and terrorizes his subjects. A method unworthy of One who perpetually invokes the Law and demands submission to it. If, as Moses Mendelssohn maintains, Judaism is not a religion but a revealed legislation, it seems strange that such a God should be its author and symbol. He who has, precisely, nothing of the legislator about Him. Incapable of the slightest effort of objectivity, He dispenses justice according to His whim, without any code to limit His divagations and His impulses. He is a despot as jittery as He is aggressive, saturated with complexes, an ideal subject for psychoanalysis. He disarms metaphysics, which detects in Him no trace of a substantial, self-sufficient Being superior to the world and content with the interval that separates Him from it. A clown who has inherited heaven and who there perpetuates the worst traditions of earth, He employs extreme means, astounded by His own power and proud of having made its effects felt. Yet His vehemence, His shifts of mood, His spasmodic outbursts finally attract, if they do not convince us. Not at all resigned to His eternity, He intervenes in the affairs of earth, makes a mess of them, sowing confusion and clutter. He disconcerts, irritates, seduces.

However eccentric He may be, He knows his charms, and uses them at will. But what is the good of listing the flaws of a God when they are displayed throughout those frenetic books of the Old Testament, beside which the New seems a thin and touching allegory? We vainly seek the former's poetry and asperity in the latter, where everything is sublime amenity, a narrative intended for "good souls." The Jews have refused to recognize themselves in it: that would be to fall into the trap of happiness, to strip themselves of their singularity, to opt for an "honorable" destiny, all things alien to their vocation. "Moses, the better to bind the nation to himself, instituted new rites, contrary to those of all other mortals. Here, all that we worship is flouted; in return, all that is impure in our eyes is allowed" (Tacitus).

"All other mortals"—this statistical argument, which antiquity certainly abused, could not escape the moderns: it has served, it will always serve. Our duty is to reverse it in favor of the Jews, to use it for the edification of their glory. Too quickly we forget that they were the citizens of the desert, that they still bear it within them as their inward space, and perpetuate it down through history, to the great amazement of those human trees, "all other mortals."

Perhaps we should add that this desert, far from constituting merely an inward space, was extended *physically* in the ghetto. Anyone who has visited one of these (preferably in an Eastern country) cannot fail to have noticed the lack of vegetation: nothing grew there, everything was dry and desolate. A strange island, the ghetto, a tiny universe *without roots*, to the measure of its inhabitants, as remote from the life of the soil as angels or ghosts.

*

"The nations feel toward the Jews," observes one of their coreligionists, "the same animosity the flour must feel toward the yeast that keeps it from resting." *Rest*, that is all we ask; the Jews may ask it too: it is forbidden them. Their febrility needles us, lashes us on, carries us away. Models of rage and bitterness, they infect us with a craving for rage and epilepsy, for aberrations which arouse us and prescribe unhappiness as a stimulant.

If the Jews have degenerated, as is commonly said, we might wish such a degeneration on all the old nations . . . "Fifty centuries of neurasthenia," Péguy said. Yes, but a daredevil's neurasthenia, not that of invalids or dyspeptics. Decadence, a phenomenon inherent in all civilizations, the Jews are ignorant of, since their career, while developing in history, has no historical essence: their evolution involves neither growth nor decrepitude, neither apogee nor decline;

their roots thrust into no one knows what soil; certainly not into our own. Nothing *natural*, vegetal in them, no *"sap,"* no possibility of withering. There is something abstract about their perenniality, but nothing bloodless—a suspicion of the demoniac, hence simultaneously unreal and active, a disturbing halo, a kind of reverse nimbus which individualizes them forever.

If they escape decadence, all the more reason for them to escape satiety, a wound from which no ancient people is safe and against which all medication turns out to be inoperative: has it not killed more than one empire, more than one soul, more than one organism? The Jews are miraculously inured against it. What could they have been satiated *by*, when they have known no respite, none of those moments of fulfillment propitious to disgust but mortal to desire, to will, to action? Unable to stop anywhere, they must desire, will, act, sustain themselves in anxiety and nostalgia. Do they fix upon an object? It will not last: every event will be for them only a repetition of the Destruction of the Temple. Memories and prospects of collapse! The ankylosis of peace does not lie in wait for them. Whereas it is painful for us to persevere in a state of avidity, they actually never emerge from it, and in it feel a kind of *morbid well-being*, suitable to a collectivity to which a state of trance is endemic and whose mystery falls within the province of theology and pathology, without, moreover, being elucidated by the combined efforts of both.

Forced to face their depths and fearing them, the Jews try to bypass, to elude them by clinging to the trifles of conversation: they talk, they talk . . . But the easiest thing in the world: to remain on the surface of the self, they never achieve. For them, speech is an evasion: sociability, a self-defense. We cannot, without trembling, imagine their silences, their monologues. Our calamities, the reverses of our life, are to them familiar disasters, routine; their image of time: a crisis overcome or a crisis to come. If by religion we mean the will of the creature to raise himself *by his discomforts*, they all have, devout or atheist, a religious tinge, a piety whose sweetness they were careful to eliminate, along with its self-satisfaction, composure, and all that might flatter the innocent, the weak, the pure. It is a piety without naiveté, for none of them is naive, as, on another level, none of them is stupid. (Stupidity, indeed, is not in circulation among them: almost all are quick-witted; those who are not, the few rare exceptions, do not stop at stupidity, they go further: they are simple-minded.)

That passive, languid prayers should not be to their taste is understandable; moreover such orisons displease their God, who contrary to ours, does not condone boredom. Only the sedentary man prays in peace, without haste; nomads, the hunted, must work fast and hurry on, even in their obeisances. This is because they invoke a God who is Himself a nomad, Himself hunted, and Who communicates to them His impatience and His panic.

When one is ready to capitulate, what a lesson, what a corrective in their endurance! How many times, when I was indulging the prospect of my ruin, have I not thought of their stubbornness, their persistence, their comforting as well as inexplicable appetite for being! I owe them many returns, many compromises with the non-evidence for living. And yet, have I always done them justice? Far from it. If at twenty I loved them to the point of regretting not being one of them, later on, unable to forgive them for having played a leading role in the course of history, I found myself loathing them with the fury of love turned to hate. The vividness of their omnipresence made me all the more sensitive to the obscurity of my country, doomed, I knew, to be smothered and even to disappear; while they, I knew just as well, would survive everything, whatever happened. Furthermore, at the time, I had only a bookish commiseration for their past sufferings, and could not divine those that were in store for them. Afterwards, thinking of their tribulations and of the resolution with which they endured them, I was to grasp the value of their example and to derive from it several reasons for struggling against my temptation to abandon everything. But whatever my feelings toward them at various moments of my life, on one point I have never varied: I mean my attachment to the Old Testament, the veneration I have always felt for *their* book, that providence of my excesses or of my ironies. Thanks to it, I communicated with them, with the best of their afflictions; thanks to it, too, and to the consolations I derived from it, so many of my nights, however inclement they may have been, seemed tolerable to me. This I could never forget, even when they seemed to me to deserve their opprobrium. And it is the memory of those nights when, by the poignant sallies of Job and Solomon, they were so often present, that justifies the hyperboles of my gratitude. Let someone else do them the insult of making "meaningful" statements about them! I cannot bring myself to do so: to apply our standards to them is to strip them of their privileges, to turn them into mere mortals, an ordinary variety of the human type. Happily, they defy our criteria as well as the investigations of common sense. To reflect on these tamers of the abyss (of *their* abyss), one glimpses the advantage of not giving over, of not yielding to the voluptuous delight of shipwreck, and by meditating their rejection of ruin, one resolves to imitate them, knowing even so that it is vain to make the attempt, that our lot is to sink down, to answer the Call of the Abyss. Nonetheless, by turning away, even temporarily, from our impulse to submit, they teach us to come to terms with a dizzying, unendurable world: they are *masters at existing.* Of all those who suffered a long period of slavery, they alone have succeeded in resisting the charms of abulia. Outlaws who hoarded their strength, by the time the Revolution gave them a civil status, they possessed more important biological resources than those of other nations. Free at last,

they appeared, in the nineteenth century, in broad daylight
and astounded the world: since the period of the conquistadors, no one had seen such intrepidity, such an awakening.
A curious, unexpected, lightninglike imperialism. Repressed
for so long, their vitality burst upon the world; and they,
who appeared so self-effacing, so humble, were suddenly at
grips with a thirst for power, for domination and glory, which
alarmed the disabused society in which they began to assert
themselves and into which these indomitable elders were to
inject new blood. Greedy and generous, insinuating themselves into every branch of commerce and knowledge, into
all kinds of enterprises, not to accumulate but to expend, to
squander; famished in repletion, prospectors of eternity
strayed into the quotidian, nailed to gold and to heaven, and
constantly mingling the luster of one with that of the other
—a luminous and alarming promiscuity, a whirlpool of ab-
jection and transcendence—they possess in their incompatibilities their true fortune. In the days they lived by usury,
were they not studying the Kabbala in secret? Money and
mystery: obsessions they have retained in their modern oc-
cupations, a complexity impossible to disentangle, a source
of power. To persecute, to combat them? Only the madman
risks doing so: he alone dares confront the *invisible* weapons
with which they are armed.

To contemporary history, inconceivable without them,
they have given an accelerated cadence, a splendid breath-
lessness, a superb second wind, as well as a prophetic poison
whose virulence has not ceased disconcerting us. Who, in
their presence, can remain neutral? One never approaches
them to waste one's time. In the diversity of the psychological landscape, each one of them is a case. And if we
know them by certain aspects, there is still a number of
steps to take before we penetrate their enigmas. Incurables
who intimidate death, who have discovered the secret of
another health, of a dangerous health, of a salutary disease,

they obsess you, torment you, and oblige you to rise to the level of their consciousness, of their vigils. While with *the others*, everything changes: beside them, one falls asleep. What security, what peace! One is at once *"entre nous,"* one yawns, one snores without fear. By such frequentations, one is converted to the apathy of the soil. Even the most refined seem peasants, boors gone wrong. They wrap themselves, poor wretches, in a comforting fatality. Even if they had genius, they would still be ordinary. A vile fate pursues them: their existence is as obvious, as acknowledged as that of the land or of the water. Subsided elements.

*

No creatures less anonymous. Without them who could breathe in our cities? They maintain a state of fever, without which any agglomeration becomes a province: a dead city is a city without Jews. Effective as a ferment and a virus, they inspire a double sense of fascination and discomfort. Our reaction to them is almost always murky: by what precise behavior are we to adjust to them, when they locate themselves both above and beneath us, on a level which is never our own? Whence a tragic, inevitable misunderstanding for which no one takes the responsibility. What madness on their part to have attached themselves to a special God, and what remorse they must feel when they turn their eyes toward our insignificance! No one will ever disentangle the web in which we are caught, each inextricably laced to the other. Should we rush to their aid? We have nothing to offer them. And what they bring us—is beyond us. Whence do they come? Who are they? We approach them with a maximum of perplexity: he who takes a clear-cut attitude toward them misunderstands them, simplifies them, and becomes unworthy of their extremities.

A remarkable thing: only the unsuccessful Jew resembles us, is "one of us": it is as if he had retreated toward ourselves, toward our conventional and ephemeral humanity.

Must we thereby deduce that man is a Jew *who has not gone all the way?*

*

Bitter and insatiable, lucid and impassioned, always in the *avant garde* of solitude, they represent failure *on the move.* If they do not sacrifice to despair when everything should incite them to do so, the reason is that they lay plans the way others breathe, that they suffer the disease of projects. In the course of a single day, each of them conceives an incalculable number. Against the grain of the dirt-choked races, they cling to the imminent, send down roots into the possible: this automatism of the new explains the effectiveness of their divagations, as well as their horror of every intellectual comfort. Whatever nation they inhabit, they are at the mind's root-tip. Collectively, they constitute a mass of exceptions, a *summa* of capacities and talents unexampled in any other nation. If they practice a profession, their curiosity is not limited by it; each possesses passions or hobbies which carry him *elsewhere,* enlarge his knowledge, permit him to embrace the most disparate professions, so that his biography implies a host of characters united by a single will—it, too, unprecedented. The notion of " ̣erservering in being" was conceived by their greatest philosopher; such being they have conquered in pitched battle. Hence their mania for plans and projects: to the subsiding present, they oppose the aphrodisiac virtues of tomorrow. *Becoming* —again, it is one of them who made it the central notion of his philosophy. No contradiction between the two ideas, process leading back to the being who projects, and projects himself; to the being disintegrated *by hope.*

But is it not vain to assert that they are this or that in philosophy? If they tend to rationalism, it is less by inclination than by a need to react against certain traditions which excluded them and from which they have suffered. Their genius, as a matter of fact, accommodates itself to any form of theory, any current of ideas, from positivism to mysticism. To emphasize only their propensity to analysis is to impoverish them, and to do them a grave injustice. They are, after all, a people who have prayed enormously. One realizes this from their faces, more or less bleached by the reading of the psalms. Then too, one meets, among them, only, *pale* bankers . . . Which must mean something. Finance and *De Profundis!*—unprecedented incompatibility, perhaps the key to their general mystery.

*

Combatants by preference—the most warlike of all civilian peoples—they proceed in their affairs as strategists, and never avow themselves defeated, though they often are. Condemned and blessed, their instinct and intelligence do not neutralize each other: even in their flaws, everything serves them as a tonic. Their progress, with its wanderings and its dizzy spells—how could it be understood by a slippered humanity? If they had, over the latter, merely the superiority of a quenchless failure, of a more successful way *of not arriving*, would that not suffice to assure them a relative immortality? Their last resort holds fast: it fails *eternally*.

Active, virulent dialecticians, stricken with a neurosis of the intellect (which far from hampering them in their enterprises, drives them on, makes them dynamic, obliges them to live under pressure), they are fascinated, despite their lucidity, by risk. Nothing makes them retreat. Tact, an earthbound vice, a prejudice of *enraciné* civilizations, the instinct of protocol—is not their strong point: the responsibility for this lies in their flayed pride, in their aggressive mind. Their irony, far from being an amusement at others' expense, a form of sociability or caprice, smells of repressed vitriol; it is a long-brewed bitterness; envenomed, its darts kill. It participates, not in the laughter which is relief but in the jeer which is the wince and revenge of the abased. Indeed, the Jews are unrivaled at jeering. To understand them, or to approach them, we must have lost, ourselves, more than one homeland, must be, like them, citizens of every city, must fight *without a flag* against the whole world, must know, after their example, how to embrace and betray every cause. A difficult task, for compared to them we are, whatever our ordeals, poor creatures swallowed up by happiness and geography, neophytes of misfortune, bunglers in every genre. If they do not possess a monopoly on subtlety, the fact remains, nonetheless, that their form of intelligence is the most disturbing there is, the *oldest*; it is as if they know everything, have always known everything, since Adam, since . . . God.

*

Do not accuse them of being parvenus: how could they be, when they have passed through and left their mark on so many civilizations? Nothing in them of the recent, the improvised: their ·promotion to solitude coincides with the dawn of History; their very defects are imputable to the vitality of their old age, to the excesses of their penetration and their acuity of mind, to their excessively long experience. They are ignorant of the comfort of limits: if they possess a wisdom, it is the wisdom of exile, the kind which teaches how to triumph over a unanimous sabotage, how to believe oneself chosen when one has lost everything: the wisdom of defiance. And yet they are called cowards! It is true that they can cite no spectacular victory: but their very existence, is that not one? An uninterrupted, terrible victory, with no chance of ever ending!

To deny their courage is to misunderstand the value, the quality of their fear, an impulse not of retraction but of expansion, the beginning of an offensive. For this fear, in contrast to the cowardly and the humble, they have converted into a virtue, a principle of pride and conquest. It is not flaccid like ours, but strong and enviable, and consists of a thousand dreads transfigured into acts. According to a recipe they have been careful not to reveal, our negative forces become, in them, positive; our torpors, migrations. What immobilizes us makes them advance, leap forward: no barrier which their itinerant panic fails to surmount. Nomads to whom space does not suffice and who, beyond continents, pursue some other homeland . . . Consider the ease with which they traverse the nations! One, born in Russia, is now a German, a Frenchman, then an American, or anything . . . Despite these metamorphoses, he retains his identity; he has character, as they all do. How explain otherwise their capacity to begin, after the worst mortifications, a new existence, to take their destiny in hand once again? It is something of a wonder. Observing them, one is amazed and stupefied. In this life, they must have had experience of hell. Such is the ransom of their longevity.

When they begin to decline, and when they seem ruined, they catch themselves up, gain ground and refuse the quietude of failure. Hunted from their homes, born expatriates, they have never been tempted to give up. But the rest of us, apprentices of exile, latter-day *déracinés*, eager to attain to sclerosis, the monotony of collapse, to an equilibrium without horizon or promise, crawl behind our misfortunes; our condition transcends us; unsuited to the terrible, we were made to languish in some imaginary Balkans, not share the fate of a legion of Singulars. Gorged on immobility, prostrate, haggard, how, with our somnolent desires and our crumbled ambitions, how could we possess the stuff the Wanderer is made of? Our ancestors, bent over the earth, scarcely detached themselves from it. Unhurried, for where would they have gone? their gait was that of the plow: the speed of eternity . . . But to enter History supposes a residue of precipitation, of impatience and of vivacity, all things different from the slow barbarism of agricultural peoples, hemmed in by Habit—that regulation not of their privileges, but of their melancholies. Scratching at the ground to be able to rest in it more easily at the end, leading a life at the level of the grave, a life in which death seemed a reward and a privilege, our ancestors have bequeathed us the legacy of their endless sleep, their mute and somewhat intoxicating desolation, their long sigh of living dead men.

We are dazed; our curse acts upon us like a narcotic: it benumbs us; that of the Jews has the value of a flick of the lash: it drives them ahead. And if they attempt to evade it? A delicate question, perhaps unanswerable. What is certain is that their sense of the tragic differs from that of the Greeks. An Aeschylus treats the misfortune of an individual or of a family. The concept of a national malediction, any more than that of a collective salvation, is not Hellenic. The tragic hero rarely seeks an accounting from a blind, impersonal Fate: it is his pride to accept its decrees. He will perish, then, he and his. But a Job harasses his God, demands an accounting: a formal summons results, of a sublime bad taste, which would doubtless have repelled a Greek but which touches, which overwhelms us. These outpourings, these vociferations of a plagued man who offers conditions to Heaven and submerges it with his imprecations—how can we remain insensitive to such a thing? The closer we are to abdicating, the more these cries disturb us. Job is indeed of his race: his sobs are a show of force, an assault. "My bones are pierced in me in the night season," he laments. His lamentation culminates in a cry, and this cry rises through the vaults of heaven and makes God tremble. Insofar as, beyond our silences and our weaknesses, we dare lament our ordeals, we are all descendants of the great leper, heirs of his desolation and his moan. But too often our voices fall silent; and though he shows us how to work ourselves up to his accents, he does not manage to shake us out of our inertia. Indeed, he had the best of it: he knew Whom to vilify or implore, Whom to attack or pray to. But we— against whom are we to cry out? Our own kind? That seems to us absurd. No sooner articulated than our rebellions expire upon our lips. Despite the echoes he wakens in us, we are not entitled to consider Job our ancestor: our pains are too timid. And our dreads. With neither the will nor the nerve to savor our fears, how can we make them into a spur or a spasm of delight? We manage to tremble; but to know how to orient our tremors is an art: all rebellions proceed from it. He who would avoid resignation must educate, must attend to his fears, and transform them into acts and words: he will be more likely to succeed if he cultivates the Old Testament, paradise of the *frisson*.

By inculcating us with the horror of extravagant language, with respect and obedience in all things, Christianity has made our fears anemic. If it sought to win us over forever, it should have treated us harshly, promised us a perilous salvation. What can we expect from a genuflection that has lasted twenty centuries? Now that we are *standing* at last, we suffer dizzy spells: slaves emancipated in vain, rebels the demon mocks or is mortified by.

Job has transmitted his energy to his own people: thirsting like him for justice, they never yield before the evidence of an iniquitous world. Revolutionaries by instinct, the notion of renunciation fails to occur to them: if Job, that Biblical Prometheus, struggled with God, they will struggle with men . . . The more fatality impregnates them, the more they revolt against it. *Amor fati*, a formula for amateurs of hero-ism, does not suit these people who have too much destiny to keep clinging to the idea of destiny . . . Attached to life to the point of seeking to remake it, and to make the impos-sible Good triumph within it, they rush upon any system likely to confirm them in their illusion. No utopia fails to blind them, to excite their fanatic zeal. Not content with having preached the idea of progress, they have even seized upon it with a sensual and almost shameless fervor. Did they expect, by adopting it without reservation, to benefit by the salvation it promises humanity in general, to profit from a universal Grace, a universal apotheosis? The truism that all our disasters date from the moment when we began to glimpse the possibility of "something better"—they will not admit. If they live in an impasse, they reject it in their thoughts. Rebelling against the ineluctable as against their miseries, they feel freer at the very moment when *the worst* should fetter their minds. What did Job hope for on his dung-heap, what do they all hope for? The optimism of the plague-stricken . . . According to an old treatise on psychiatry, they furnish the highest percentage of suicides. If this were true, it would prove that for them life deserves the effort to cut oneself off from it, and that they are too attached to it to be able to despair *to the end*. Their strength: rather make an end of everything than accustom oneself to, or delight in, despair. They assert themselves at the very moment they destroy themselves, in so great a horror do they hold surrender, release, the confession of lassitude. Such intensity must come from on high. I cannot explain it to myself otherwise. And if I entangle myself in their contradictions and wander, lost, through their secrets, I understand at least why they have always intrigued religious minds, from Pascal to Rozanov.

Have we thought enough about the reasons why these out-casts eliminate death from their thoughts, death the dominant idea of all exiles, as if, between them and it, there were no point of contact? Not that it leaves them indifferent, but in the course of banishing death from their minds they have managed to take a deliberately superficial attitude toward it. Perhaps, in remote ages, they granted it too much concern for death to bother them now; perhaps they do not think of it because of their quasi-imperishability: only ephemeral civilizations willingly chew the cud of nothingness. Whatever the reason, they have only life before them . . . And that life which, for the rest of us, is summed up in a formula: "Everything is impossible" and whose last word is flatteringly addressed to our failures, our abasement or our sterility—that life awakens in them a preference for the obstacle, a horror of deliverance and of any form of quietism. These warriors would have stoned Moses if he had addressed them in the language of a Buddha, the speech of metaphysical lassitude, offering annihilation and salvation. Neither peace nor beatitude for the man who cannot cultivate abandon: the absolute, as the suppression of all nostalgia, is a reward enjoyed only by those who force themselves to lay down their arms. Such a recompense disgusts these impenitent soldiers, these volunteers of malediction, this people of Desire . . . By what aberration have we ever referred to their love of destruction? They—destroyers? Rather we should reproach them with not being destructive enough. For how many of *our* hopes are they not responsible! Far from conceiving demolition in itself, if they are anarchists, they always seek some future creation, some construction, impossible, perhaps, but craved. Then too, it would be a mistake to minimize the pact, unique of its kind, which they have concluded with their God, and of which all of them, atheists or not, retain the memory and the mark. This God, however we may strive against Him, is nonetheless present, carnal and relatively effective, as any tribal God should be, whereas ours, more universal, hence more anemic, is, like any spirit, remote and inoperative. The Old Covenant, far more solid than the New, if it permits the sons of Israel to advance in concert with their turbulent Father, keeps them, in exchange, from appreciating the intrinsic beauty of destruction.

They make use of the notion of "progress" to combat the corrosive effects of their lucidity: it is their calculated evasion, their *willed* mythology. Even they, even these clearsighted minds, recoil before the last consequences of doubt. One is truly skeptical only if one stands outside one's fate or if one renounces having a fate altogether. They are too engaged in theirs to be able to escape it. There is no Indifference among them—did they not introduce interjections into religion? Even when they permit themselves the luxury of being skeptics, theirs is the skepticism of embittered hearts. Solomon suggests a ravaged and lyrical Pyrrho . . . Thus the most disabused of their ancestors, thus all of them. With what complacency they display their sufferings and open their wounds! This masquerade of confidences is only a way of *hiding*. Indiscreet and yet impenetrable, they escape you even when they have told you all their secrets. A being who has suffered, no matter how much you have described, classified, explained his ordeals, eludes you in what he *is*, in his real suffering. The closer you come to him, the more inaccessible he will seem. As for this *stricken* collectivity, you can examine their reactions at your leisure, you will nonetheless find yourself confronting a mass of unknowns.

*

However luminous their minds, a subterranean element resides in them: they appear, they burst forth, these ubiquitous, remote beings always on the *qui-vive*, fleeing danger and soliciting it, rushing upon each sensation with the hysteria of the condemned, as if they had no time to wait and as if the Terrible lay in wait for them upon the very threshold of their delights. Happiness they cling to, taking advantage of it without restraint or scruple, as if they were encroaching upon other men's possessions. Too ardent to be Epicurians, they poison their pleasures, devour them, set about them with a haste, a frenzy which keeps them from affording the least solace: men of affairs in every sense of the word, from the most vulgar to the noblest. The obsession of *afterwards* plagues them; yet the art of living—the apanage of non-prophetic ages, that of Alcibiades, of Augustus, or of the Regent—consists in the integral experience of the present. Nothing Goethean in them: they never seek to arrest the moment, even the loveliest. Their prophets, who constantly call down the thunders of God, who demand that the enemy's cities be annihilated, know how to talk *ashes*. It is their madness that must have inspired Saint John to write the most admirably obscure book of antiquity. Issuing from a mythology of slaves, the *Apocalypse* represents the best-camouflaged settling of accounts that can be imagined. In it, everything is prosecution, bile, and a pernicious future. Ezekiel, Isaiah, Jeremiah had certainly prepared the ground . . . Skilled at making the most of their disorders or their visions, they raved with an art never equalled since: their powerful and imprecise minds helped them in the task. For them, eternity was a pretext for convulsions, a spasm: vomiting imprecations and anthems, they wriggled before the eyes of a God insatiable for hysterias. This was a religion in which man's relations with his Creator are exhausted in a war of epithets, in a tension which keeps him from pondering, from emphasizing and thereby from remedying his differences, a religion based on adjectives, effects of language, and in which style constitutes the only hyphen between heaven and earth.

*

If these prophets, fanatics of the dust, poets of disaster, always predicted catastrophes, it was because they could not attach themselves to a reassuring present or a commonplace future. On the pretext of turning their people from idolatry, they poured out their rage, tormented them and sought to make them as frenzied, as terrible as themselves. Hence they had to harry, to singularize that people by ordeal, keep it from constituting, from organizing itself as a mortal nation . . . By cries and threats, they succeeded in making it acquire that authority in *angst* and that look of a vagrant, insomniac horde which irritates the natives and disturbs their snores.

*

If someone were to object that they are not exceptional by their nature, I should reply that they are so by their destiny, an absolute destiny, a destiny in the pure state, which by conferring strength and excess raises them above themselves and strips them of all capacity to be mediocre. One might also object that they are not the only ones to define themselves by destiny, that the same is true of the Germans. No doubt; yet we forget that the destiny of the Germans, if they have one, is recent, and that it comes down to the tragic quality of a period; as a matter of fact, to two close-set failures.

These two peoples, secretly drawn to one another, could never reach an understanding: how could the Germans, those arrivistes of fatality, forgive the Jews for having a destiny superior to their own? Persecutions are born of hatred, not of disdain; and hatred is equivalent to a reproach one dares not make to oneself, to an intolerance with regard to our own ideal embodied in others. When we aspire to leave our province behind and dominate the world, we attack those who are no longer bound by any frontier: we resent their facility in uprooting themselves, their ubiquity. The Germans detested in the Jews their dream *realized*, a universality they could not achieve. They too wanted to be chosen: nothing predestined them to that condition. After having attempted to force History, with the motive of escaping and transcending it, they ended by sinking even deeper into it. Henceforth, losing all chance of ever rising to a metaphysical or religious destiny, they were to founder in a monumental and useless drama, without mystery or transcendence, one which, leaving the theologian and the philosopher indifferent, interests only the historian. Had they been more difficult in the choice of their illusions, they would have afforded us another example than that of the greatest, the first of the ineffectual nations. He who chooses time is engulfed by it and buries his genius therein. One *is* chosen; one becomes so neither by resolve nor by decree. Still less by persecutions of those whose complicities with eternity one envies. Neither chosen nor damned, the Germans pursued those who could rightfully claim to be: the culminating moment of their expansion will count, in the distant future, only as an episode in the epic of the Jews . . . I repeat, the epic, for what else is it, that succession of prodigies and exploits, that heroism of a tribe which, amid its miseries, ceaselessly threatens its God with an ultimatum? An epic whose *dénouement* is not to be divined: will it be fulfilled *elsewhere?* or will it take the form of a disaster which escapes the perspicacity of our terrors?

*

A fatherland—*heimat, patrie*—is a moment-by-moment soporific. One cannot sufficiently envy—or pity—the Jews for not having one, or for having only provisional ones, Israel first of all. Whatever they do and wherever they go, their mission is to keep watch; this is the command of their immemorial status as aliens. A solution to their fate does not exist. There remain the arrangements with the Irreparable. Hitherto, they have found nothing better. This situation will last until the end of time. And it is to this situation that they owe the mishap of not perishing . . .

*

In sum, though attached to this world, they do not really belong to it: there is something non-terrestrial in their passage on earth. Were they in far-off times the witnesses of a spectacle of beatitude for which they retain a certain nostalgia? And what must they have *seen* then which eludes our perceptions? Their penchant for utopias is merely a memory projected into the future, a vestige converted into an ideal. But it is their fate, even as they aspire to Paradise, to collide with the Wailing Wall.

Elegiac in their fashion, they dope themselves with regrets, believe in them, make them into a stimulant, an auxiliary, a means of conquering, by the detour of history, their first, their ancient happiness. It is upon that happiness they rush, it is toward it they run. And that race lends them an expression, both spectral and triumphant, which terrifies and seduces us, laggards that we are, resigned in advance to a mediocre destiny and forever incapable of believing in the *future* of our regrets.

SOME BLIND ALLEYS:
A LETTER

I HAD always supposed, dear friend, that loving your province as you do, you were resolved upon the practice, there, of detachment, scorn, silence. Imagine, then, my surprise on hearing you say you were preparing a book about it! Instantaneously, I saw looming up within you a future monster: the author you will become. "Another one lost," I thought. Modestly, you refrained from asking the reasons for my disappointment; and I should have been incapable of giving them *viva voce*. "Another one lost, another one ruined *by his talent*," I kept murmuring to myself.

Penetrating the literary inferno, you will come to learn its artifices and its arsenic; shielded from the immediate, that caricature of yourself, you will no longer have any but formal experiences, indirect experiences; you will vanish into the Word. Books will be the sole object of your discussions. As for literary people, you will derive no benefit from them. But you will find this out too late, after having wasted your best years in a milieu without density or substance. The literary man? An indiscreet man, who devaluates his miseries, divulges them, tells them like so many beads: immodesty—the side-show of second-thoughts—is his rule; he *offers himself*. Every form of talent involves a certain shamelessness. Only sterility is truly distinguished—the man who effaces himself along with his secret, because he disdains to parade it: sentiments *expressed* are an agony for irony, a slap at humor.

To keep one's secret is the most fruitful of activities. It torments, erodes, *threatens* you. Even when confession is addressed to God, it is an outrage against ourselves, against the mainspring of our being. The apprehensions, shames, fears from which both religious and profane therapeutics would deliver us constitute a patrimony we should not allow ourselves to be dispossessed of, at any cost. We must defend ourselves against our healers and, even if we die for it, preserve our sicknesses and our sins. The confessional? a rape of conscience perpetrated in the name of heaven. And that other rape, psychological analysis! Secularized, prostituted, the confessional will soon be installed on our street corners: except for a couple of criminals, everyone aspires to have a public soul, a poster soul.

Drained by his fecundity, a phantom who has worn out his shadow, the man of letters diminishes with each word he writes. Only his vanity is inexhaustible; if it were psychological, it would have limits: those of the self. But it is cosmic or demonic: it submerges him. His "work" obsesses him; he continually alludes to it, as if, on our planet, there were nothing outside himself which deserved attention or curiosity. Woe to anyone with the impudence or bad taste to discuss anything but his productions! You will understand, then, how one day, leaving a literary luncheon, I saw the necessity for a Saint Bartholomew's Day Massacre of men of letters.

Voltaire was the first literary man to erect his incompetence into a procedure, a method. Before him, the writer, content to be tangent to events, was more modest: plying his trade in a limited sector, he followed his own nose and kept it clean. Nothing of the journalist about him, at most he was interested in the anecdotic aspect of certain solitudes: his indiscretion was *ineffectual*.

With our braggart, things change. None of the subjects which intrigued his times escaped his sarcasm, his half-knowledge, his craving for controversy, his universal vulgarity. In Voltaire, everything was impure except his style . . . Profoundly superficial, without any sensibility for the *intrinsic*, for the interest reality offers in itself, he inaugurated in letters our ideological gossip. His mania for chatter, for indoctrinating, his porter's-lodge wisdom, were to make him the prototype, the model of the *littérateur*. Since he said everything about himself, and since he exploited to the last drop the resources of his nature, he no longer troubles us: we read him and move on. On the other hand, in the case of a Pascal we feel sure he has not told us all there is to say; even when he irritates us, he is never, for us, *an author*.

To write books is to have a certain relation with original sin. For what is a book if not a loss of innocence, an act of aggression, a repetition of our Fall? To publish one's taints in order to amuse or exasperate! A barbarism with respect to our intimacy, a profanation, a defilement. And a temptation. I know what I am talking about, and I speak—advisedly. At least I have the excuse of hating my actions, of performing them without believing in them. You are more honest: you will write books and you will believe in them, you will believe in the reality of words, in those childish and indecent fictions. From the depths of my disgust, everything literary looks to me like a chastisement; I shall try to forget my life for fear of discussing it; or else, unable to accede to that absolute of disillusion, I shall condemn myself to a morose frivolity. Shards of instinct, nonetheless, compel me to cling to words. Silence is unbearable: what strength it takes to settle into the concision of the Inexpressible! It is easier to renounce bread than speech. Unfortunately, the verbal turns to verbiage, to literature. Even thought that way tends, ever ready to spread out, to puff up; to check it with a period, to contract it into an epigram or a witticism is to counter its expansion, its natural movement, its impulse toward dilution, toward inflation. Whence our systems, whence our philosophies. This obsession with brevity paralyzes the mind's progress, for the mind needs words *en masse*, without which, turned upon itself, it ruminates upon its impotence. If thinking is an art of repeating, of discrediting the essential, it is because the mind is a pedant. And an enemy of any form of wit, of all those who are obsessed with paradox and arbitrary definitions. Horrified by banality, by "the universally valid," they address themselves to the accidental side of things, to matters "obvious" to no one. Preferring an approximative but piquant formula to an evident but insipid reasoning, they aspire to no particular accuracy and amuse themselves at the expense of "truths." Reality does not hold up—why should they take seriously the theories that try to prove its solidarity? In everything, they are paralyzed by the fear of boring or of being bored. This fear, if you are subject to it, will comprise all your undertakings. You try to write; immediately there looms up before you the image of your reader . . . And you lay down your pen. The notion you want to develop is too much for you: what is the use of examining it, of getting to the heart of the matter? Couldn't a single phrase, a formula translate it? Besides, how set forth what you already know? If you are obsessed by a verbal economy, you can neither read nor reread any book without detecting its artifices and its redundancies. You finally discover that even the author you continually return to pads his sentences, hoards pages and collapses on an idea in order to flatten it, to stretch it out. Poem, novel, essay, play—everything seems too long. The writer—it is his function—always says more than he has to say: he swells his thought and swathes it with words. All that subsists of a work are two or three *moments*: lightning in the lumber rom. Shall I tell you what I really think?

Every word is a word *de trop*. Yet the question is: to write. Let us write . . . , let us dupe each other.

Boredom dismantles the mind, renders it superficial, out at the seams, saps it from within and dislocates it. Once ennui has seized you, it will accompany you to every encounter, as it has accompanied me for as long as I can remember. I know no moment when it was not here, beside me, in the air, in my words and in those of others, on my face and on all faces. It is both mask and substance, façade and reality. I cannot imagine myself, living or dead, without it. Boredom has made me into a speechifier ashamed of raising his voice, a theoretician for the senile and the adolescent, for metaphysical menopauses, a vestige of a creature, a hallucinated clown. Whatever share of Being was dispensed to me is being eroded by ennui, and if a few scraps remain it is only because boredom requires some substance on which to act . . . The Void in action, it ransacks brains and reduces them to a heap of fractured concepts. No idea which it leaves *in touch* with any other, which it fails to isolate and grind down, so that the mind's activity is debased into a series of discontinuous moments. Notions, sentiments, sensations in tatters, such is the effect of its passage. It would make a saint into an amateur, a Hercules into a rag. Boredom is a sickness that extends *farther* than space; you must flee it, or entertain merely meaningless projects, like mine when it drives me to the wall. I dream then of an acid thought which might insinuate itself into things and disorganize them, perforate them, come out the other side—of a book whose syllables, attacking the paper, would suppress literature and readers alike, of a book that would be both carnival and apocalypse of Letters, an ultimatum to the pestilence of the Word.

I find it hard to understand your ambition to make a name for yourself in an age when the epigone is *de rigueur*. A comparison is inevitable. On the philosophical and literary level, Napoleon had rivals who were his equals: Hegel by the excess of his system, Byron by his unbuttoned liberty, Goethe by a mediocrity *without precedent*. Today, it would be futile to elicit the literary pendant to the adventurers, the tyrants of the century. If, politically, we have given proof of an unprecedented insanity, in the domain of the mind only tiny destinies fidget; no conqueror *by the pen:* nothing but monsters, hysterics, simply *cases*. We do not have, and I fear never shall have, the *oeuvre* of our undoing, a Don Quixote in hell. The more the times distend, the more literature shrinks. And it is as pygmies that we shall be engulfed by the Unparalleled.

Judging from appearances, in order to revive our aesthetic illusions we require an *askesis* of several centuries, an ordeal by silence, an age of non-literature. For the moment, it remains for us to corrupt every genre, to drive them to the extremes which deny them, to undo what was marvelously done. If, in this enterprise, we show some concern for perfection, perhaps we shall manage to create a new type of vandalism . . .

Placed outside of style, incapable of harmonizing our debacles, we no longer define ourselves in relation to Greece: it has ceased to be our guideline, our nostalgia or our remorse; it has been extinguished within us . . . But so has the Renaissance.

From Hölderlin and Keats to Walter Pater, the nineteenth century was able to oppose its opacities and to counter them with the image of a mirific antiquity, a cure by light—in short, Paradise. A forged paradise, it goes without saying. What matters is that it was aspired to, even if only to combat modernity and its grimaces. One could devote oneself to another age, and cling to it with all the violence of regret. The past still *functioned*.

We no longer have a past; or rather, there is nothing left of the past which is our own; no longer a chosen country, no lying salvation, no refuge in yore. Our prospects? Impossible to disentangle them: *we are barbarians without a fu-*

ture. Expression not being of a stature to measure itself against events, to fabricate books and appear proud of doing so constitutes a spectacle eminently pathetic: what necessity impels a writer who has produced fifty books to write still one more? Why this proliferation, this fear of being forgotten, this debased coquetry? Only the literature of need deserves our indulgence these days, produced by the slave, the drudge of the pen. In any case, there is no longer anything *to construct*, neither in literature nor philosophy. Only people who live by them, materially I mean, should take them up. We are entering a period of broken forms, of creations in reverse. Anyone can flourish now. I am scarcely anticipating. Barbarism is accessible to all: it is sufficient to develop a taste for it. Blithely, we shall dissolve the centuries.

What your book will be, I can guess only too well. You live in the provinces: insufficiently corrupted, possessed of pure anxieties, you are unaware how much any "sentiment" dates. The inner drama is reaching its end. How dare a man venture once again upon a work that begins with the "soul," with a prehistoric infinite?

And then, there is the matter of tone. Yours—I'm afraid —will be of the "noble," "reassuring" variety, tainted with common sense, proportion, or elegance. Get it through your head that a book should address itself to our incivism, to our singularities, to our lofty turpitudes, and that a "humane" writer who sacrifices to ideas which are too acceptable signs his own literary death warrant.

Examine the minds which manage to intrigue us: far from taking the way of the world into consideration, they defend *indefensible* positions. If they are lifelike, at least, it is thanks to their limitations, to the passion of their sophistries: the concessions which they have made to "reason" disappoint us, irritate us. Discretion is deadly to genius; ruinous to talent. You will understand, dear friend, why I have apprehensions about your complicities with the "humane."

As though to give yourself a certain "positive" assurance, which harbored as well a suspicion of superiority, you have often reproached me for what you call my "appetite for destruction." You should know that I destroy nothing: I record, I record the *imminent*, the thirst of a world which is canceling itself out and which, upon the wreck of its appearances, races toward the unknown and the incommensurable, toward a spasmodic style. I know one mad old woman who expects her house to fall to pieces from one minute to the next; she spends her days and her nights on the alert; creeping from room to room, ears cocked for every sound, she is furious that the *event* takes so long to occur. In a larger context, the old woman's behavior is our own. We count on a collapse, even though we do not think about it. It will not always be this way; one can even foresee that the fear of ourselves, result of a more general fear, will constitute the basis of education, the principle of future pedagogies. I believe in the future of the terrible. You, my dear friend, are so little prepared for it that you are about to enter literature. I have no qualifications to discourage you; at least I should like you to proceed without illusions. Temper the author champing within you, adopt for your own, with suitable enlargement, this remark of Saint John Climacus: "Nothing procures so many crowns for the monk as discouragement."

If, upon further reflection, I have shown some complacency in destroying, it was, contrary to what you think, always at my own expense. One does not destroy, save as one destroys *oneself*. I have hated myself in all the objects of my hatreds, I have imagined miracles of annihilation, pulverized my hours, tested the gangrenes of the intellect. Initially an instrument or a method, skepticism ultimately took up residence inside me, became my physiology, the fate of my body, my visceral principle, the disease I can neither cure nor die of. I incline—it is only too true—toward things stripped of any chance of ending or surviving. So you will understand why I have always been concerned with the

West. This concern seemed to you absurd or gratuitous. "The West—you aren't even part of it," you pointed out. Is it my fault if my greed for misery has not found another object? Where else will I find so persistent a will to fail? I envy the West the dexterity with which it manages to die out. When I would fortify my disappointments, I turn my mind toward this theme of an inexhaustible negative richness. And if I open some history of France, England, Spain, or Germany, the contrast between what they were and what they are gives me, besides a certain vertigo, the pride of having discovered, at last, the axioms of twilight.

I am far from trying to pervert your hopes: life will take care of that. Like everyone else, you will proceed from one forfeiture to the next. At your age, I had the advantage of knowing some people in a position to initiate me, to make me blush for my illusions; they truly educated me. Without them, should I have had the courage to face or to endure the years? By imposing *their* bitterness, they prepared me for my own. Armed with great ambitions, they set out to conquer some glory or other. Failure awaited them. Delicacy, lucidity, sloth? I could not tell you which virtue cut across their plans. They belonged to that category of individuals whom one meets in capital cities, living by expedients, always looking for a situation they reject as soon as it is found. From their remarks I learned more than from all the rest of my associations. Most of them carried a book inside them, the book of their setbacks; tempted by the demon of literature, they nonetheless withstood it, so subjugated were they by their defeats, so full of disaster were their lives. They are commonly called "failures." They form a type of man apart, which I shall attempt to describe to you, at the risk of simplifying him. A voluptuary of fiasco, he seeks his own diminution in everything, never gets past the preliminaries of his future, nor crosses the threshold of any enterprise. Rivaling the angels in *abulia*, he meditates upon the secret of action, and takes but one initiative: that of abandon. His faith, if he has any, serves him as a pretext for new capitulations, for a degradation glimpsed and longed for: he collapses into God . . . If he reflects upon the "mystery," it is to show others to what lengths he carries his indignity. He inhabits his convictions like a worm in the fruit; he founders with them and recovers only to rouse against himself whatever melancholies he has left. If he smothers his gifts, it is because he so loves his lassitude; he advances toward his past, retraces his steps *in the name of his talents.*

You will be surprised to learn that he proceeds in this way only because he has adopted a rather odd attitude with regard to his enemies. Let me explain. When we are in the mood to be effective, we know that our enemies cannot keep us from placing ourselves at the center of their attention and of their interest. They prefer us to themselves, they take our affairs to heart. In our turn we are concerned with them, we watch over their health, as over their hatred, which alone permits us to sustain a few illusions about ourselves. They save us, belong to us—they are our own. With regard to his enemies, *the failure* reacts differently. Not knowing how to preserve them, he ends up losing interest in them, minimizing them, no longer taking them seriously. A detachment with the gravest consequences. In vain will he attempt, later, to goad them on, to waken the slightest curiosity about him, to provoke their indiscretion or their rage; in vain, too, will he attempt to rouse them to pity his condition, to conserve or quicken their rancor. With no one *against whom* to affirm himself, he will be imprisoned in solitude and sterility. A solitude and a sterility I prized so highly among these defeated men responsible, as I have said, for my education. Among others, they revealed to me the stupidities inherent in the cult of Truth . . . I shall never forget my comfort when it ceased to be my business. A master of every error, I could at last explore a world of appearances, of frivolous enigmas. Nothing more to pursue, except the pursuit of nothing. The Truth? An adolescent fad or a symptom of senility. Yet out of some trace of nostalgia or some craving for slavery, I still seek it, unconsciously, stupidly. A second's inattention is enough for me to relapse into the oldest, the most absurd of prejudices.

I am destroying myself, certainly; meanwhile, in this asthmatic climate that convictions create in a world of oppressed men, I breathe; I breathe in my fashion. Some day, who knows? you may experience this pleasure of aiming at an idea, firing at it, seeing it there, prone, before you, and then beginning the exercise again on another, on all; this longing to lean over someone, to divert him from his old appetites, his old vices, in order to impose new and more noxious ones upon him, until he dies of them; to set yourself against an age or a civilization, to fling yourself upon time and martyrize its moments; then to turn against yourself, to torment your memories and your ambitions and, destroying your breath, to infect the air in order to suffocate all the better . . . , some day perhaps you will know this form of breathing which is deliverance from self and from everything. Then you will be able to commit yourself to anything without adhering to it.

*

My purpose was to put you on guard against the Serious, against that sin which nothing redeems. In exchange, I wanted to offer you . . . futility. Now—why conceal it?—futility is the most difficult thing in the world, I mean a futility that is conscious, acquired, deliberate. In my presumption, I hoped to achieve it by the practice of skepticism. Yet skepticism adapts itself to our character, follows our defects and our passions, even our follies; skepticism personalizes itself. (There are as many skepticisms as there are temperaments.) Doubt waxes by all that weakens or opposes it; it is a sickness within another sickness, an obsession within obsession. If you pray, it rises to the level of your prayer; it oversees your delirium, even as it imitates it; in the middle of your vertigo, you will doubt—vertiginously. Thus, to abolish the Serious, skepticism itself is of no avail; nor, alas, is poetry. The older I grow, the more I realize that I have counted too much on poetry. I have loved it at the expense of my health; I anticipated succumbing to my worship of it. Poetry! the word itself once led me to imagine a thousand universes and now no longer wakens in my mind anything but a vision of singsong and nullity, of fetid mysteries and affectations. It is only fair to add that I have made the mistake of frequenting a good number of poets. With very few exceptions, they were uselessly solemn, infatuated, or odious, monsters, specialists, tormentors, and martyrs of the adjective whose dilettantism, lucidity, and intellectual sensibility I had vastly overestimated. Is futility, then, no more than an "ideal"? That is what I must fear, that is what I shall never be resigned to. Each time I catch myself assigning some importance to things, I incriminate my mind, I challenge it and suspect it of some weakness, of some depravity. I try to wrest myself from everything, to raise myself by uprooting myself; in order to become futile, we must sever our roots, must become metaphysically *alien*.

In order to justify your ties, and as though impatient to bear the burden of them, you claimed one day that it was easy for me to float, to flourish in thin air because, coming from a country without history, nothing *weighed* upon me. I acknowledge the advantage of belonging to a minor country, of living without a background, with the unconcern of a tumbler, an idiot or a saint, or with the detachment of that serpent which, coiled around itself, survives without food for years on end, as if it were some god of inanition or else concealed, beneath the suavity of its hebetude, some hideous sun.

Without any tradition to encumber me, I cultivate a curiosity about that displacement which will soon be the universal fate. By will or by force, we shall all suffer an historical eclipse, the imperative of confusion. Already we are being canceled out in the sum of our divergences from ourselves. By constantly denying itself, our mind has lost its center, diffused in *attitudes*, in metamorphoses as futile as they are inevitable. Whence the indecency and the mobility of our behavior. Our unbelief and even our faith are marked by it.

To attack God, to seek to dethrone Him, to supplant Him, is an exploit in bad taste, the performance of an envious man who takes a vain satisfaction in coming to grips with a unique and uncertain Enemy. Whatever form it takes, atheism presumes a lack of manners, as does, for converse reasons, apologetics; for is it not an indelicacy as well as a hypocritical charity, an impiety to do battle in order to sustain God, to assure Him, whatever the cost, a—longevity? The love or the hate we bear Him reveals not so much the quality of our anxieties as the grossness of our cynicism.

We are responsible for this state of affairs only in part. From Tertullian to Kierkegaard, by accentuating the absurdity of faith, Christianity has created an undercurrent which, now appearing in broad daylight, has overflowed the Church. What believer, in his fits of lucidity, does not consider himself a servant of the Irrational? God was to suffer for it. Hitherto we granted Him our virtues; we dared not lend Him our vices. Humanized, He resembles us now: none of our defects is alien to Him. Never have the broadening of theology and the thirst for anthropomorphism been carried so far. This modernization of Heaven marks its end. How can we venerate an advanced God, an up-to-date God? To His misfortune, He will not soon recover His "infinite transcendence."

"Beware," you might argue, "beware what you call a 'failure of manners.' You are only denouncing atheism the better to sacrifice to it."

Upon myself I am only too aware of the stigmata of my time: I cannot leave God in peace; along with the snobs, I entertain myself by repeating that He is dead, as if that had any meaning. By such impertinence we hope to despatch our solitudes, and the supreme phantom which inhabits them. In reality, as they increase they merely bring us closer to what haunts them.

When Nothingness invades me and, according to an Oriental formula, I attain to the "vacuity of the void," it so happens that, crushed by such an extremity, I fall back on God, if only out of a desire to trample my doubts underfoot, to contradict myself and, multiplying my *frissons*, to seek in Him a stimulant. The experience of the Void is the unbeliever's mystic temptation, his possibility for prayer, his moment of plenitude. At our limits, a God appears, or something that serves his turn.

*

We are far from literature: but far only in appearance. These are only words, sins of the Word. I recommended to you the dignity of skepticism: here I am prowling around the Absolute. A technique of contradiction? Recall, instead, Flaubert's words: "I am a mystic and I believe in nothing." I see it as the adage of our age, of an age infinitely intense, and without substance. There exists a voluptuousness which is all our own: the voluptuousness of conflict *as such*. Convulsive minds, fanatics of the improbable, drawn between dogma and aporia, we are as ready to leap into God *out of rage* as we are resolved not to vegetate in Him.

Only the professional heretic, the man rejected by vocation, is contemporary, at once the spew and panic of our orthodoxies. In the past, you were defined by the values to which you subscribed; today, by those you repudiate. Without the pomp of negation, man is a pauper, a lamentable "creator," incapable of fulfilling his destiny as a capitalist of collapse, an amateur of the crash. Wisdom? Never was any period so free of it—in other words, never was man more himself: a being refractory to wisdom. A traitor to zoology, an animal *astray*, man rebels against nature, even as the heretic against tradition. The heretic is thus man to the second degree. Every innovation is his doing. His passion: to find himself at the origin, at the point of departure of anything and everything. Even when he is humble, he aspires to make others feel the effects of his humility and believes that a religious, philosophical, or political system is worth the trouble of being broken or renewed: to put oneself at the heart of a rupture is all he asks. Hating equilibrium and the sluggishness of institutions, he shoulders them aside to hasten their end.

The wise man, the sage, is hostile to the new. Disabused, he abdicates: that is his form of protest. Proud enough to isolate himself in the *norm*, he asserts himself by *retreat*. To what does he aspire? To surmount or neutralize his contradictions. If he succeeds, he proves that they lacked vigor, that he had transcended before truly facing them. Instinct failing, it is easy for him to be master of himself, to pontificate in the anemia of his serenity.

Once we are carried away by ourselves, we realize that it is not in our power to stop, to cool off our contradictions or conjure them away. They guide us, stimulate us and kill us. The sage, rising above them, accommodates himself to them, does not suffer from them, *gains* nothing by dying. In other periods, he was a model; for us, he is no more than a failure of biology, an anomaly without attraction.

You defame wisdom, because you cannot accede to it, because it is "forbidden" you, you may be thinking. In fact it is certain that is what you are thinking. To which I answer that it is too *late* to be wise, that in any case it would serve no purpose, for the same abyss will engulf us all, wise and foolish alike, sane and mad. I acknowledge, moreover, that I am the sage I shall never be . . . Every formula for salvation acts upon me like a poison: it defeats me, augments my difficulties, aggravates my relations with others, irritates my wounds and, instead of exercising a salutary virtue upon the economy of my days, plays a mortal role in them. Yes, every wisdom acts upon me like a *toxin*. No doubt you are also thinking that I am too much "in step" with this age, that I am making too many concessions to it. In fact, I applaud and deny it with all the passion and incoherence I possess. It gives me the sensation of a last act, hypostatized. Must we deduce from this that it will never end, that this interminable coda will merely perpetuate its incompletion? Nothing of the kind. I foresee what will happen, and to enhance such knowledge we need merely reread Saint Jerome's letter after the sack of Rome by Alaric. It expresses the astonishment and the uneasiness of a man who, from the periphery of an empire, contemplates its disintegration and its inertia. Consider this document: it is your epitaph, anticipated. I do not know if it is legitimate to speak of the end of man; but I am certain of the fall of all the fictions by which we have lived until today. Let us say that history is finally revealing its night side, and, to remain in the realm of the unspecific, that a world is destroying itself. Well then, in the hypothesis that I alone can keep this from happening, I shall make no gesture, I shall not raise my little finger. Man attracts and appalls me, I love and hate him with a vehemence which condemns me to passivity. I cannot imagine how to go about saving him from his fatality. How naive we must be to blame or defend him! Lucky those who entertain toward him a clear and distinct sentiment: they will perish *saved*.

To my shame, I confess that there was a time when I too belonged to that category of happy beings. Man's fate touched me to the quick, though in another fashion. I must have been about twenty, your age. "A humanist" in reverse, I supposed—in my still intact pride—that to become the enemy of the human race was the highest dignity to which one might aspire. Eager to cover myself with ignominy, I envied all who exposed themselves to the world's sarcasm and spittle and who, accumulating shame upon shame, missed no occasion for solitude. I came thus to idealize Judas because, refusing to endure any longer the anonymity of dedication, he sought to singularize himself by treason. It was not out of venality, I chose to think, but ambition that he *gave Jesus away*. He dreamed of equaling him, of counterbalancing him in evil; in good, with such a competitor, there was no way for Judas to distinguish himself. Since the honor of being crucified was forbidden him, he was able to make the tree of Aceldama a replica of the Cross. All my thoughts followed him on the road to that hanging, while I too prepared to sell my idols. I envied his infamies, the courage it took to make himself execrated. What a torment to be ordinary, a man among men! Turning to the monks meditating night and day on their seclusion, I imagined them mulling over crimes and outrages that were more or less aborted. Every solitary, I told myself, is suspect: a *pure* being does not isolate himself. To seek the intimacy of a cell, one must have a heavy conscience; one must be afraid of one's conscience. I regretted bitterly that the history of monasticism had been undertaken by straightforward minds, as incapable of conceiving the need to be odious to oneself as of experiencing that melancholy which moves mountains . . . A raving hyena, I anticipated making myself hateful to every creature, forcing them to league together against me, crushing them or being crushed by them. In other words, I was ambitious . . . Since then, by dint of modulations, my illusions were to lose their virulence and creep modestly toward disgust, ambiguity, and bewilderment.

*

At the end of these deliberations, I cannot help repeating that it is hard for me to discern the place you seek to occupy in our time; in order to inscribe yourself within the age, have you enough flexibility, enough of a thirst for inconsistency? Your sense of balance presages nothing very helpful here. As you are, you have a long way to go. In order to liquidate your past, your innocence, you require an initiation into vertigo. Simple enough for those who understand that fear, grafted onto matter, causes it to make that leap of which we are in a sense the final reverberation. There is no such thing as time, there is only that fear which develops and disguises itself as moments . . . , which is here, inside us and outside us, omnipresent and invisible, the mystery of our silences and our screams, of our prayers and our blasphemies. Now, it is precisely in the twentieth century that this fear is approaching its apogee, full blown, proud of its conquests and its successes. Neither our frenzies nor our cynicism had hoped for as much. And it is no longer surprising that we are so far from Goethe, the last citizen of the cosmos, the last grand *naif*. His "mediocrity" joins nature's. The least *déraciné* of minds: a friend of the elements. Opposed to all that he was, for us it is a necessity and almost a duty to be unfair to him, to shatter him within us, to shatter *ourselves* . . .

If you lack the power to demoralize yourself along with the age, to go as low and as far, do not complain of being misunderstood by it. Above all, do not suppose yourself to be a precursor: there will be no "light" in this century. Hence if you insist upon contributing some innovation, prospect your nights or despair of your career.

In any case, do not accuse me of having used a peremptory tone with you. My convictions are pretexts: what right do I have to impose them on you? The same is not true of my vacillations; those I do not invent, I believe in them, I believe in them despite myself. Hence it is in good faith, and regretfully, that I have inflicted upon you this lesson in perplexity.

STYLE AS RISK

INURED to a purely verbal art of thinking, the sophists were the first to occupy themselves with a meditation upon words, their value, propriety, and function in the conduct of reasoning: the capital step toward the discovery of style, conceived as a goal in itself, as an intrinsic end, was taken. It merely remained to transpose this verbal quest, to assign as its object: the harmony of the sentence, to substitute for the play of abstraction the play of expression. The artist reflecting on his means is therefore indebted to the sophist and organically related to him. Both pursue, in different directions, the same genre of activity. Having ceased to be *nature*, they live as a function of the word. Nothing original in them: no link that binds them to the sources of experience; no naiveté, no "sentiment." If the sophist thinks, he so dominates his thought as to do with it what he likes; since he is not carried away by it, he directs it according to his caprice or his calculation; he treats his own mind as a tactician; he does not meditate, he conceives, according to a plan as abstract as it is artificial, certain intellectual operations, opens a breach in concepts, proud to reveal their weakness or to grant them, arbitrarily, a solidity or a sense. "Reality" is not his concern: he knows it depends on the signs which express it and which must, simply, be mastered.

The artist, too, proceeds from the word to the actual: *expression* constitutes the only original experience of which he is capable. Symmetry, arrangement, the perfection of certain formal operations represent his natural milieu; he lodges there, breathes there. And since he aims at exhausting the capacity of words, he tends, more than to expression, to *expressiveness*. In the closed universe he inhabits, he escapes sterility only by that continuous renewal afforded by a game in which nuance acquires idolatrous dimensions and in which a verbal chemistry achieves compounds inconceivable to a naive art. So deliberate an activity, if it is located at the antipodes of *experience*, approaches, on the other hand, the extremities of intellect. It makes the artist who dedicates himself to it a sophist of literature.

In the life of the mind, there occurs a moment when style, transforming itself into an autonomous principle, becomes fate. It is then that the Word, as much in philosophical speculations as in literary productions, reveals both its vigor and its void.

A writer's manner is conditioned physiologically; he possesses a rhythm of his own, urgent and irreducible. One does not conceive a Saint-Simon changing the structure of his sentence nor condensing his prose, tending to laconicism by the effect of a willed metamorphosis. Everything in him required that profusion of interlinked, luxuriant, mobile phrases. The imperatives of syntax must have pursued him like a torment and an obsession. His breath, its cadence, even its catches, imposed that fluid and ample movement which surmounts the solitude and the barrier of words. There was in him a *pedal point* so different from those flute accents which characterize French. Whence those periods which, dreading the *period*, overrun each other, multiply digressions, refuse to end.

In contrast, think of La Bruyère, his way of cutting the sentence, restricting, halting it, careful to delimit its confines: the semicolon is his obsession; he has punctuation in his soul. His opinions, even his sentiments are *placed*. He is reluctant to solicit them, fears irritating or exasperating them. Since he is short-winded, the lineaments of his thought are distinct; he prefers to remain within rather than transcend his nature. Whereby he espouses the genius of a language which has specialized in the sighs of the intellect, a language for which whatever is not cerebral is suspect or null. Condemned to dryness by its very perfection, unfit to assimilate and translate the Iliad and the Bible, Shakespeare and Don Quixote, cleared of any affective charge and somehow exempt of its origin, French is closed to the primordial and the cosmic, to all that precedes or transcends man. But the Iliad, the Bible, Shakespeare, or Don Quixote participate in a kind of naive omniscience, which is located both beneath and above the human phenomenon. The sublime, the horrible, blasphemy or outcry—French approaches them only in order to denature them by rhetoric. It is no better adapted to delirium, nor to raw humor: Achilles and Priam, David, Lear, or Don Quixote are smothered under the rigors of a language which makes them appear boorish, pitiful, or monstrous. However different they may be, they all live—and this is their common feature—on the level of the *soul*, which for its expression requires a language faithful to the reflexes, linked to instinct, not disincarnate.

*

After having frequented certain idioms whose plasticity gave him the illusion of an unlimited power, the unbridled foreigner, loving improvisation and disorder, tending toward excess or equivocation by an inaptitude for clarity, if he approaches French with timidity, sees it nonetheless as an instrument of salvation, an *askesis* and a therapeutics. By practicing it, he cures himself of his past, learns to sacrifice a whole background of obscurity to which he was attached, simplifies himself, becomes *other*, desists from his extravagances, surmounts his old confusions, increasingly accommodates himself to common sense, to reason; besides, can one lose reason and still wield a tool which requires its exercise, even its abuse? How can one be mad—or a poet—in such a language? All its words seem aware of the signification they translate: lucid words. To use them for poetic ends is equivalent to a gamble or a martyrdom.

"As lovely as . . . prose"— a French joke if there ever was one. The universe reduced to the articulations of the sentence, *prose as the unique reality*, the word self-absorbed, emancipated from the object and from the world: a sonority-in-itself, cut off from the exterior, the tragic ipseity of a language bound to its own finitude.

*

When we consider the style of our times, we cannot help wondering about the reasons for its corruption. The modern artist is a solitary who writes for himself or for a public of which he has no precise notion. Linked to an epoch, he struggles to express its features; but this epoch is necessarily *faceless*. He does not know whom he is addressing, he does not imagine his reader. In the seventeenth century and the one following, the writer had in view a small circle whose requirements he knew, as well as its degree of finesse and acuity. Limited in his possibilities, he could not depart from the rules, real though unformulated, of taste. The censorship of the salons, more severe than that of today's critics, permitted the flowering of perfect and minor geniuses, constrained to elegance, to the miniature and the finite.

Taste is formed by the pressure the idle exert upon Letters, especially in epochs when society is refined enough to set the tone for literature. When we realize that once upon a time a mangled metaphor discredited a writer, that an academician lost face for an impropriety, or that a witticism uttered in a courtesan's hearing could procure a situation, even an abbey (such was Talleyrand's case), we measure the distance that has been covered since. The terrorism of taste has ceased, and with it the superstition of style. To bemoan the fact would be as ridiculous as it is ineffectual. Behind us lies a sufficiently solid tradition of vulgarity; art must adapt, must resign itself to it or be isolated in an absolutely subjective expression. To write for everyone or for no one— each man decides the matter for himself, according to his nature. Whatever choice we make, we are sure of no longer meeting on our way that old scarecrow, a failure of taste.

*

Virus of prose, a poetic style dislocates and wrecks it: poetic prose is sick prose. Moreover, it always dates: the metaphors one generation affects appear absurd to the next. If we read a Saint-Evremond, a Montesquieu, a Voltaire, a Stendhal as if they were our contemporaries, it is because they sinned neither by lyricism nor by excess of images. Since prose participates in the *procès-verbal*, the report of the evidence, the prose-writer must conquer his first impulses, forbid himself the temptation of sincerity: all faults of taste come from the "heart." The *people* inside us bears the responsibility for our excesses, our extravagances: what is more plebeian than a sentiment?

The sum of imperceptible constraints, the sense of gauge and proportion, a vigilance maintained over our faculties, a modesty with regard to words, *taste* is the characteristic of authors who, untouched by the mania of being "profound," sacrifice some of their power for the sake of a certain anemia. One cannot, it goes without saying, find it in our century. It is forever past, that age when one could be marvelously superficial. The decadence of the exquisite assured that of style which, as soon as it is picturesque, complex, breaks down under the weight of its own richness. Whose fault, if it is one? Perhaps we should blame romanticism; but even romanticism was no more than the consequence of a general deterioration, an effort of liberation *at the expense of the exquisite*. To tell the truth, the eighteenth century's refinement could not have been perpetuated without falling into stereotype, affectation, or sclerosis.

*

A nation going downhill diminishes in every domain. "Every individual or national degradation," Joseph de Maistre observes, "is immediately heralded by a strictly proportional degradation in the language itself." Our deficiencies stain our style; as for a nation, its increasingly shaky instinct drags it into an equivalent uncertainty in all realms. France, for over a century, has abandoned her old idea of perfection. The same was true for Rome: the eclipse of her power was contemporary with the decline of Latin which, docile in the service of doctrines and chimeras opposed to its genius, became a tool monopolized by the Councils. The language of Tacitus, distorted, trivialized, forced to endure divagations on the Trinity! Words have the same destiny as empires.

In the age of the salons, French acquired a dryness and a transparency which allowed it to become universal. When it began to grow complicated, to take liberties, its solidity suffered. The language freed itself at last to the detriment of its universality and, like France, is evolving toward the antipodes of its past, of its genius. A double and inevitable disintegration. In the age of Voltaire, each man tried to write like everyone; but everyone wrote perfectly. Today, the writer wants his own style, to individualize himself by expression; he succeeds only by destroying his language, violating its rules, undermining its structure, its magnificent monotony. This process is one it would be foolish to attempt to avoid; we contribute to it in spite of ourselves, and it must be so, on pain of literary death. From the moment French declines, let us declare ourselves a part of its destiny, let us profit by the profundities it displays, as by its insistence on prevailing over the modesty of its limits. Nothing more futile than to expostulate against its lovely autumn, its Indian summer. Let us try to rejoice, rather, at living in an age when words, used in any sense, free themselves from all constraint, and when meaning no longer constitutes a demand or an obsession. No doubt about it: we are attending the splendid disintegration of a language. Its future? Perhaps it will know a few spasms of delicacy or, more likely, will end by serving in the modern Councils, worse than those of antiquity. A rapid death-agony could just as well be its fate. Whether or not it is on its way to a vestigial state, the fact remains that we see more than one of its words losing what remained of its vitality. Will the genius of prose leak into other idioms?

*

A nation of words, France has asserted herself by the scruples she conceived in their regard. Of these scruples there remain certain traces. A magazine, drawing up the balance sheet of the half-century in 1950, cited the major event of each year: end of the Dreyfus Affair, the Kaiser's visit to Tangiers, etc. . . . For 1911, it notes simply: "Faguet admits the '*malgré que*' construction." Has such solicitude ever been granted elsewhere to the Word, to its daily life, to the details of its existence? France has cherished words to the point of vice, and at the expense of *things*. Dubious of our possibilities of knowing, she is not so of our possibilities of *formulating* our doubts, so that she identifies our truths with the mode of translating our mistrust of them. In every delicate civilization there functions a radical disjunction between reality and the word.

To speak of decadence in the absolute signifies nothing; linked to a literature and to a language, it concerns only the man who feels himself attached to one and the other. Is French deteriorating? The only person to be alarmed about it will be the one who sees it as a unique and irreplaceable instrument. It matters little to him that in the future another, more manageable, less exigent idiom might be found. When one loves a language, it is a dishonor to survive it.

For two centuries, all originality has been manifested by an opposition to classicism: no new form or formula has not reacted against it. To pulverize the *acquired,* such seems to me the essential tendency of the modern mind. In whatever sector of art you consider, every style asserts itself against *style.* It is by undermining the idea of reason, of order, of harmony that we gain consciousness of ourselves. Romanticism, to come back to it once again, was merely an impulse toward a more fecund dissolution. The classical universe no longer being viable, we must shake it up, introduce into it a suggestion of incompletion. "Perfection" no longer troubles us: the rhythm of our life renders us insensitive to it. To produce a "perfect" work, one must be able to *wait,* to live within that work until it supplants the universe. Far from being the product of a tension, it is the fruit of a passivity, the result of energies accumulated over a long period of time. But we expend ourselves, we are men without reserves; and with that, incapable of being sterile, having entered the automatism of creation, fit for any work of any kind, for all half-successes.

*

"Reason" is dying not only in philosophy, but also in art. Too perfect, Racine's characters seem to belong to a world scarcely conceivable to us. Even Phèdre seems to be insinuating: "Look at my beautiful suffering. I defy you to suffer its equal!" We no longer suffer that way; our logic having changed face, we have learned to do without the evidence. Whence our passion for the vague, the imprecision of our progress and of our skepticism: our doubts are no longer defined in relation to our certitudes, but in relation to other, more *consistent* doubts, which we must render a little more supple, a little more fragile, as if our purpose, unconcerned with the establishment of a truth, was to create a hierarchy of fictions, a scale of errors. As for the "truth," we hate its limits and all that it represents as a bridle to our whims, to our race for the new. Indeed the classical artist, digging ever deeper in a single direction, despised the new, despised all originality for its own sake.

We want space at all costs, even if the mind must sacrifice its laws there, its old requirements. What little *evidence* we must have in spite of everything we do not really believe in: simple *points de repère*. Our theories, like our attitudes, are animated by our sarcasm. And this sarcasm, the root of our vitality, explains why we advance dissociated from our footsteps. All classicism finds its laws in itself and abides by them: it lives in a present without history; while we are living in a history which keeps us from having a present. Thus, not only our style but our time itself is a broken one. We have not been able to break it without, in a parallel direction, breaking our thought: in a perpetual squabble with themselves, our ideas, ready to cancel each other out, to fly into splinters—our ideas crumble like our time.

*

If there is a relation between a writer's physiological rhythm and his manner, there is *a fortiori* a relation between his temporal universe and his style. The classical writer, citizen of a linear, delimited time whose frontiers he never crossed—how could *he* have produced a jerky, jarring style? He saved up words, lived on them *at home*. And these words reflected for him the eternal present, that tense of perfection which was his own. But the modern writer, no longer having a resting place in time, must affect a convulsed, epileptic style. We may regret that such is the case and acrimoniously evaluate the ravages which the overthrow of the old idols involves. Still, the fact is that it is impossible to adhere still to an "ideal" style. Our mistrust of the "phrase" touches a whole region of literature: the one which relied on "charm," which employed the methods of seduction. Those writers who still resort to it baffle us, as if they were trying to perpetuate a superannuated world.

Every idolatry of style starts from the belief that reality is even more hollow than its verbal figuration, that the accent of an idea is worth more than the idea, a well-turned excuse more than a conviction, a skillful image more than an unconsidered explosion. It expresses a sophist's passion, the passion of a sophist of Letters. A well-proportioned sentence, satisfied with its equilibrium or swollen with its sonority, all too often conceals the *malaise* of a mind incapable of acceding by *sensation* to an original universe. What is surprising if style should be simultaneously a mask and an admission?

BEYOND THE NOVEL

THERE was a time when the artist mobilized all his defects to produce a work which *concealed himself*; the notion of exposing his life to the public probably never occurred to him. We do not imagine Dante or Shakespeare keeping track of the trifling incidents of their lives in order to bring them to other people's attention. Perhaps they even preferred giving a false image of what they were. They had that reticence of power which is no longer a property of the deficient modern. Our confessions, our novels are all characterized by the same aberration. What interest can a mere life afford? What interest, books inspired by other books or minds dependent on other minds? Only the illiterate have given me that *frisson* of being which indicates the presence of truth. Carpathian shepherds have made a much deeper impression upon me than the professors of Germany, the wits of Paris. I have seen Spanish beggars, and I should like to have been their hagiographer. They had no need to invent a life for themselves: they *existed*; which does not happen in civilization. Why, one wonders, didn't our ancestors barricade themselves in their caves?

When the average man lays claim to a destiny, then the average man can describe his own. The belief that psychology reveals our essence necessarily endears our actions to us: we imagine they possess an intrinsic or symbolic value. Then comes the snobbery of "complexes" which teaches us to exaggerate our blanks, to be dazzled by them, to gratify our ego with faculties and depths it is obviously unendowed with. The intimate perception of our nothingness, however, is only partially veiled by this process. We suspect that the novelist who relies on his life is only pretending to believe in it, that he has no respect for the secrets he discovers there: he is not taken in, and we, his readers, are still less so. His characters belong to a second-rate humanity, conscious and contaminated, suspect on account of their artifices, their intrigues. We do not readily conceive of an *astute* Lear . . . The vulgar, the parvenu aspect of the novel determines its characteristics: fatality cheapened, destiny in lower case, agony improbable, tragedy *déclassé*.

Compared with the tragic hero, so rich in the adversity that is his eternal patrimony, the novel's central character seems like a naive candidate for ruin, horror's cheap-jack, overeager to destroy himself, terrified to fail. He suffers from the very uncertainty of his disaster. There is no necessity for his death. We sense that the author could have saved him; which makes us uncomfortable, spoils our pleasure as readers. Whereas tragedy occurs on an absolute level, so to speak: the author has no influence over his heroes, he is only their servant, their instrument; they are the ones in control, and they prompt him to institute proceedings against themselves. They *rule*, even in the works for which they serve as a pretext. And these works affect us as realities independent of both the writer and the marionette-strings of psychology. We read novels in an altogether different way. The novelist is always uppermost in our minds; his presence haunts us; we watch him struggle with his characters; in the long run, he is the only one who holds our attention. "What's he going to do with them? How will he get rid of them?" we wonder, our curiosity tinged with apprehension. If someone once said that Balzac rewrote Shakespeare using failures, what can we think of today's novelists, obliged as they are to deal with a humanity that has deteriorated still further? Bereft of the cosmic afflatus, the novel's inhabitants diminish and cannot manage to counterbalance the dissolving effect of their knowledge, their will to lucidity, their lack of "character."

The appearance of the *intelligent artist* constitutes the modern phenomenon *par excellence*. Not that those of the past were incapable of abstract thought or of subtlety; but, from the start ensconced in the center of their work, they created without too much thought for the process, without surrounding themselves by doctrines and considerations of method. The art, new still, *carried* them. It does so no longer. However reduced his intellectual means, today's artist is above all an aesthetician: situated outside his inspiration, he prepares it, confines himself to it deliberately. If he is a poet, he provides a commentary for his works, explains them without convincing us, and, in order to invent, to renew himself, apes the instinct he no longer has: the idea of poetry has become his poetic material, his source of inspiration. He celebrates his poem; a fatal lapse, a poetic absurdity: poems are not made out of poetry. Only the suspect artist starts from art; the true artist draws his material elsewhere: from himself . . . Next to the contemporary "maker" with his sufferings and his sterility, the creators of the past seem embarrassingly healthy: they were not made anemic by philosophy. Question any painter, novelist, composer: you will discover there are *problems* which obsess him, affording him the insecurity that is his essential characteristic. He gropes his way as if he were condemned to halt at the threshold of his undertaking or of his fate. These days no one escapes this exacerbation of the intellect and its corresponding diminution of instinct. The monumental, the spontaneously grandiose is no longer possible; on the other hand, the *in-*

teresting is raised to the level of a genre. It is the individual who creates art, no longer art which creates the individual, just as it is no longer the work that counts, but the commentary that precedes or follows it. And the best thing an artist produces now are his ideas on what he might have done. He has become his own critic, as the average man has become his own psychologist. No age has been so self-conscious. Seen from this point of view, the Renaissance looks barbarous, the Middle Ages prehistoric, and it is only the last century which does not seem a little childish. We know a great deal about ourselves; on the other hand, we *are* nothing. Compensating for our failures of naiveté, of spontaneity, hope, and stupidity, the "psychological sense" that is our greatest acquisition has transformed us into spectators of ourselves. Our greatest acquisition? Granted our metaphysical incapacity, yes, for it is the only sort of profundity we are sensitive to. But if we transcend psychology, our entire "inner life" assumes the quality of an emotional meteorology whose variations furnish no meaning whatsoever. Why be interested in the behavior of ghosts, in the stages of appearance? And how, after *The Past Recaptured*, appeal to a self, how stake anything further on our secrets? It is not Eliot but Proust who is the prophet of the "hollow men." Take away those functions of our memory by which it attempts to triumph over time, and nothing is left inside us save the rhythm marking the degrees of our deliquescence. At this point, to refuse our annihilation is a kind of bad manners. The creaturely state is no help at all, Proust tells us as well as Meister Eckhart; with the former, we achieve the ecstasy of the void through time; with the latter, through eternity. A psychological void; a metaphysical void: the one, the crown of introspection; the other, of meditation. The "self" constitutes the privilege only of those who do not follow themselves as far as they can go. Yet this extremity, productive for the mystic, is disastrous for the writer. We do not conceive of Proust surviving his work, outlasting the vision which concludes it. Further, he has made all research in the direction of psychological detail superfluous, annoying. Ultimately, the hypertrophy of analysis hampers both the novelist and his characters. We cannot complicate to infinity a character or the situations in which he finds himself involved. We know them all, at least we guess them all.

There is only one thing worse than boredom, and that is the fear of boredom. And it is this fear I experience each time I open a novel. I have no use for the hero's life, don't attend to it, don't even believe in it. The genre, having squandered its substance, no longer has an object. The character is dying out, the plot too. It is no accident that the only novels deserving of interest today are precisely those novels in which, once the universe is disbanded, nothing happens. Even the author seems missing from them. Deliciously unreadable, with no beginning or end, they could just as well stop with the first sentence as continue for ten thousand pages. Here one question comes to mind: can the same experiment be repeated indefinitely? Why not write a novel without a subject, but why write ten or twenty? Once the necessity of absence is established, why multiply this absence—why revel in it? The implicit conception of this sort of art opposes to the erosion of being the inexhaustible reality of nothingness. Logically valueless, such a conception is nonetheless true affectively (to speak of nothingness in any other terms than affective ones is a waste of time). It postulates a research without points of reference, an experiment pursued within an unfailing vacuity, a vacuity experienced through sensation, as well as a dialectic paradoxically frozen, motionless, a dynamism of monotony and emptiness. Is this not going around in circles? *Ecstasy of non-meaning*: the supreme impasse. The manipulation of anxiety not in order to convert absence into mystery, but mystery into absence. A non-mystery, caught in its own toils and without a background, incapable of carrying the artist who conceives it beyond the revelations of absurdity.

To the narrative which suppresses what is narrated, an object, corresponds an *askesis* of the intellect, a meditation *without content* . . . The mind discovers itself reduced to the action by virtue of which it is mind and nothing more. All its activities lead it back to itself, to that stationary development which keeps it from catching on to *things*. No knowledge, no action: the meditation without content represents the apotheosis of sterility, of refusal.

The novel that deserts time abandons its specific dimension, renounces its functions: a heroic gesture it is ridiculous to repeat. Are we entitled to extenuate our own obsessions, to exploit them, endlessly resift them? More than one contemporary novelist reminds me of a mystic who has *transcended* God. Having reached this point—that is, nowhere—the mystic can no longer pray, since he has passed beyond the object of his prayers. But why do the novelists who have transcended the novel persist in writing them? So great is the novel's capacity for fascination that it subjugates even the writers who do everything in their power to get rid of it. What can translate our modern obsession with history and psychology better than the novel? If man exhausts himself in his temporal reality, he is only a character, a subject for a novel, nothing more. In fact, one of us. Moreover, the novel would have been inconceivable in a period of metaphysical prosperity: we can hardly imagine it flourishing in the Middle Ages, or in classical Greece, India, or China. For the metaphysical experience, abandoning the chronology and modalities of our being, lives in the intimacy of the absolute, an absolute toward which the individual must strive without ever achieving it: on this condition alone he may have a destiny which, to be effective in literature, supposes an incomplete metaphysical experience: I might add, voluntarily incomplete. I have in mind, of course, the Dostoevskian heroes: unqualified to save themselves, impatient for their ruin, they intrigue us insofar as they maintain a *false* relation with God. Sanctity is for them only a pretext for laceration, a supplementary chaos, a detour that permits them a superior collapse. If they actually possessed it they would cease being characters: they pursue it in order to repulse it, to enjoy the danger of falling back into themselves. It is as a saint *manqué* that the epileptic prince situates himself within a plot, for *realized* sanctity is contradictory to the art of the novel. As for Aliosha, more angel than saint, his purity does not evoke the notion of a destiny, and it is difficult to see how Dostoevsky could have made him the central figure of a sequel to the *Brothers Karamazov*. Projection of our horror of history, the angel is the reef, if not the death of narrative. Then are we to infer that the narrator's domain must not extend to the antecedents of the Fall? This seems to me singularly true for the novelist, whose function, merit, and unique *raison d'être* is to counterfeit hell.

*

I do not claim the honor of being unable to read a novel through; I simply rebel against its insolence, the addiction it has imposed upon us and the place it has assumed in our preoccupations. Nothing is worse than our endless discussions about this or that fictional character. Let me make myself clear: the most disturbing books I have ever read, if not the greatest, have been novels. Which does not keep me from loathing the vision responsible for them: a loathing without hope. For if I aspire to another world, to any world but our own, I still know I shall never achieve it. Each time I try to identify myself with some principle superior to my "experiences," I have to admit that the latter are of greater interest to me than the former, that all my metaphysical inclinations come up short against my frivolity. Right or wrong, I have come to blame the whole genre for this state of affairs, fastening my fury upon it, seeing in the novel an obstacle to myself, the agent of disintegration—my own and other people's, too—a stratagem of Time to infiltrate our substance, the final proof that eternity will never be anything more for us than a word and a regret. "Like everyone else, you're a child of the novel"—that is my refrain, and my defeat.

Attack is merely the desire to free oneself from infatuation or to punish oneself for it. I shall never forgive myself for being inwardly nearer the first novelist I meet at a party than the idlest sage of antiquity. Our passion for the rubbish of Western civilization, a civilization of the novel, has its penalties. Overshadowed by its literature, our culture grants the writer something of the same credit antiquity attributed to the philosopher. Yet the patrician who purchased his Stoic, his Epicurean, was thereby enabled to reach a level to which the bourgeois who reads his novel cannot pretend. To the objection that the philosopher of antiquity, when he was not an impostor, expatiated on themes as hackneyed as destiny, pleasure or pain, I reply that this sort of mediocrity seems to me preferable to our own, and that even the charlatanry of wisdom has more truth in it than the fabrication of novels. And as for charlatanry, let us not forget the worthier, more genuine kind—the charlatanry of poetry.

So far as we know, poetry cannot be made out of just anything: it does not always lend itself. It has its scruples and a certain . . . *standing*. To steal its substance involves certain risks: nothing could be flimsier transplanted into narrative. We are familiar with the bastard character of the novel drawing its inspiration from the romantic, symbolist, or surrealist schools. As a matter of fact, the novel, a usurper by vocation, has not hesitated to appropriate methods belonging to essentially poetic movements. Impure by its very adaptability, it has lived, it *lives* by fraud and pillage, has sold itself to every cause: it is the streetwalker of literature. What shame could embarrass it, what intimacy would it hesitate to betray? It forages in ashcans and consciences with equal ease. The novelist, whose art consists of auscultation and apocrypha, transforms our reticence into gossip columns. Even as a misanthrope he has a passion for what is human:

he wallows in it. What a pathetic figure he cuts beside the mystics with their madness, their "inhumanity!" And then, after all, God is of a different class. We can conceive of bothering about Him. But I cannot comprehend our attachment to beings. I dream of the depths of the *Ungrund*, the reality anterior to the corruptions of time, and whose solitude, superior to God, will forever separate me from myself and from my kind, from the language of love, from the prolixity that results from our curiosity about other people. If I attack the novelist, it is because, working on whatever material comes to hand, on us all, he is and must be more talkative than we. On one point, let us do him justice: he has the courage of dilution. His productivity, his power are won at that price. There is no epic talent without a science of banality, without the instinct for the inessential, for the accessory and the minute. Page after page, for pages and pages: the accumulation of inconsequence. If the catalog poem is an aberration, the catalog novel, the *roman-fleuve*, was inscribed in the very laws of the genre. *Words, words, words* . . . Hamlet must have been reading a novel.

To reflect life in all its details, to corrupt our stupefactions into anecdotes—what torture for the mind! Yet this is the torture the novelist does not feel, any more than he feels the insignificance and the naiveté of the "extraordinary." Is there a single occurrence that is worth the trouble of telling about it? A preposterous question, for I have read as many novels as the next man. But a sensible question, once time fades from our consciousness and nothing in us is left but a silence that rescues us from other beings, and from that extension of the inconceivable to the sphere of each instant by which we define existence.

*

Meaning is beginning to date. We do not spend much time in front of a canvas whose intentions are plain; music of a specific character, unquestionable contours, exhausts our patience; the over-explicit poem seems . . . incomprehensible. The dynasty of intelligibility is drawing to its close: what self-evident truth deserves the effort of being stated? What can be communicated is not worth lingering over. Are we to infer that only "mystery" can arrest our attention? It is no less tiresome than the obvious. I mean mystery in the *full* sense of the word, as it has been conceived until our own time. *Our* mystery, purely formal, is the last resort of minds disillusioned by clarity, a hollow profundity that is a match for the stage of art where no one is fooled, where, in literature, in music, in painting, we are contemporaries of every style. Eclecticism, if it wounds inspiration, widens horizons, permits us to take advantage of all traditions. It liberates the theoretician but paralyzes the creator, to whom it opens perspectives that are too vast: the work of art is produced alongside or outside of knowledge. If today's artist takes refuge in obscurity, it is because he can no longer create with *what he knows.* The extent of his information has turned him into a commentator, an Aristarchus without illusions. To safeguard his originality he has no recourse save an excursion into the unintelligible. He will therefore abandon the facts inflicted on him by an erudite and barren age. If he is a poet, he discovers that none of his words, in its legitimate acceptation, has a future; if he wants them to be viable, he must fracture their meaning, court *impropriety.* In the world of Letters as a whole, we are witnessing the capitulation of the Word which, curiously enough, is even more exhausted than we are. Let us follow the descending curve of its vitality, surrender to its degree of overwork and decrepitude, espouse the process of its agony. Paradoxically, it was never so free before; its submission is its triumph: emancipated from reality, from experience, it indulges in the final luxury of no longer expressing anything except the ambiguity of its own action. And the genre we are concerned with was to feel the repercussions of this agony, this triumph.

The advent of the novel without a subject, without *ma-*

terial, has delivered a death-blow to the novel. No more plot, characters, complications, causality. Matter excommunicated, the event abolished, only a self still survives, recalling that it once existed, a self *without a future,* clutching at the Indefinite, turning it this way and that, converting it into a tension which achieves only itself: ecstasy on the frontier of Letters, litany and soliloquy of the Void, transformation into a fugitive extremity that pursues neither the lyricism of invective nor that of prayer. Venturing to the roots of the Vague, the novelist becomes an archeologist of absence, exploring the strata of what does not and cannot exist, unearthing the imperceptible, revealing it to our accessory and disconcerted eyes. An unconscious mystic? No such thing; for the mystic, if he describes his inner torments, focuses his expectation on an object within which he manages to anchor himself. His tension is directed beyond itself or maintains itself within God, where it finds a prop and a justification. Reduced to itself, without the substructure of a reality, it would be spurious, of interest only to psychology. We must concede that the kind of reality which supports and transfigures the mystic's expectation may be illusory: by his attacks of *acedia,* the mystic admits as much. Yet such are his resources, such the automatism of his tension that instead of surrendering to the Indefinite and dissolving within it, he gives it substance, body, and countenance. Abjuring his failures, converting his waking nights into a Way, not a hypostasis, he enters a region where he no longer has the sensation (the most painful of all) that *being* is forbidden him, that a pact between it and himself will never be possible. The novelist, on the contrary, knows only the periphery, the boundaries of being: that is why he is a writer. At his best moments, he explores the no man's land that stretches between these frontiers and those of literature. Having reached this point, psychology, for lack of content, having no object to apply itself to—psychology cancels itself out, for it has entered a zone incompatible with its functioning. Imagine a novel in which the characters no longer live in terms of each other, nor of themselves, an Adolphe, an Ivan Karamazov, or a Swann without partners: you will realize why the novel's days are numbered and why, if it persists, it must content itself with a cadaver's career.

We must doubtless go further still: to the point of hoping, beyond the termination of one genre, for that of all the rest, that of art itself. Deprived of all his loopholes, man would have the good taste, by proclaiming his destitution, to stop short in his tracks, even if only for a few generations. Before beginning himself again, he would have to regenerate himself by amazement: a task in which all contemporary art engages him, insofar as the latter subscribes to its own destruction.

Not that we need believe in the future of metaphysics, or in a future of any kind. I am far from any such lunacy. The fact remains, nevertheless, that every termination conceals a promise, discloses a horizon. When we no longer see a single novel in bookstore windows, a step will have been made—perhaps forward, perhaps back . . . At least an entire civilization based on prospecting futilities will succumb. Utopia? Delirium? Barbarism? I do not know. But I keep thinking about that last novelist.

When, toward the end of the Middle Ages, the epic began to droop and die out, contemporaries of its decline must have heaved a sigh of relief; certainly they breathed more freely. Once Christian and chivalric mythology was exhausted, heroism conceived on the cosmic and divine level gave way to tragedy: Renaissance man took his limits, his destiny into his own hands, becoming himself to the point of explosion. Then, unable to endure this oppression of the sublime for long, he stooped to the novel, epic of the bourgeois era—a stand-in epic.

Before us lies a gap that will be filled by philosophic succedanea, cosmogonies full of smoky symbolism, uncertain visions. The mind will be enlarged by them, will swallow more material than it is accustomed to contain. Recall the Hellenistic period and its effervescence of gnostic sects: the Empire, with its huge curiosity, embraced irreconcilable systems and by naturalizing Oriental gods ratified a number of doctrines and mythologies. Just as an exhausted art becomes permeable to the forms of expression which once were alien to it, so a form of worship at the end of its resources permits itself to be invaded by all the rest. This was the meaning of antiquity's syncretism, this is the meaning of our own. Our emptiness, in which disparate arts and religions are heaped, appeals to idols from elsewhere, for our own are too decrepit to protect us now. Though we are specialists in other skies, we gain no advantage from them: product of our blanks, of the lack of a life principle, our knowledge is a universality of surface, a dispersion which prefigures the coming of a world consolidated in the gross and the terrible. We know how, in antiquity, dogma put an end to the fantasies of gnosticism; we can guess in what certitude our own encyclopedic aberrations will conclude. Failure of a period which substitutes for art the history of art, for religion that of religions.

*

Let us not be needlessly bitter: certain failures are sometimes fruitful. Such as the novel's. Let us salute it, then, even celebrate it: our solitude will be reinforced, affirmed. Cut off from one more channel of escape, up against ourselves at last, we are in a better position to inquire as to our functions and our limits, the futility of having a life, of becoming a character or of creating one. The novel? A veto opposed to the explosion of our appearances, the point furthest from our origins, an artifice to disguise our real problems, a screen between our primordial realities and our psychological fictions. We shall never be able to admire enough all those who, imposing techniques that deny it, atmospheres that cripple it, requirements beyond its means, vie for its ruin and for that of our age, of which it is the image, the quintessence and the grimace as well. The novel translates our every face, assumes all our possibilities of expression. Many adopt it though their natures are scarcely inclined in its direction. Today, Descartes would probably be a novelist; Pascal certainly. A genre becomes universal when it seduces minds which have no reason to embrace it. But, ironically, it is just such minds that are sapping the novel from within: they introduce problems heterogeneous to its nature, diversify it, pervert and overburden it until they make its architecture crack. If the future of the novel is not close to your heart, it should please you to see a philosopher writing one. Whenever philosophers insinuate themselves into Letters, it is to exploit their confusion or to precipitate their collapse.

*

That literature should be destined to perish is possible and even desirable. What use is the comedy of our questions, our problems, our anxieties? Would it not be preferable, after all, to orient ourselves toward a condition of automatons? Our crushing individual agonies would be succeeded by mass-produced agonies, uniform and easy to endure; no more original or profound works, no more intimacy, therefore no more dreams and no more secrets. Happiness, misery would lose all meaning, since they would have no place to start *from*; each of us would at last be ideally null and perfect: *no one*. Here in the twilight of Destiny's last days . . . let us contemplate our drifting gods: they were no worse than we, poor things. Perhaps we shall survive them, perhaps they will return diminished, disguised, furtive. Giving justice where justice is due, let us admit that if they came between us and the truth, now that they are leaving we are no closer to truth than when they forbade us to look it in the face . . . As wretched as they, we continue working in the realm of fiction, substituting, quite properly, one illusion for another: our highest certitudes are merely *functioning* lies . . .

Be that as it may, the material of literature grows thinner every day, and that of the novel, more limited, vanishes before our very eyes. Is it really dead, or only dying? My incompetence keeps me from making up my mind. After asserting that it was finished, remorse assails me: what if the novel were still alive? In that case, I leave it to others, more expert, to establish the precise degree of its agony.

DEALING WITH THE
MYSTICS

NOTHING is more irritating than those works which "co-ordinate" the luxuriant products of a mind that has focused on just about everything except a system. What is the use of giving a so-called coherence to Nietzsche's ideas, for example, on the pretext that they revolve around a central motif? Nietzsche is a sum of attitudes, and it only diminishes him to comb his work for a will to order, a thirst for unity. A captive of his moods, he has recorded their variations. His philosophy, a meditation on his whims, is mistakenly searched by the scholars for the constants it rejects.

The obsession with a system is no less suspect when it is applied to the study of the mystics. It will do, possibly, in the case of a Meister Eckhart, who took the trouble to discipline his thought: was he not a preacher? A sermon, however inspired, partakes of the *course*, sets forth a thesis, and labors to reveal its cogency. But what can we say of an Angelus Silesius, whose distichs readily contradict one another and possess only one theme in common: God—presented in so many aspects that it is difficult to identify the true one? *The Cherubic Wanderer*, a series of irreconcilable remarks, a splendor of confusion, expresses only the strictly subjective states of its author: to try to detect its unity, its system, is to spoil its capacities for seduction. Angelus Silesius is preoccupied less with God than with his own god. A host of poetical insanities are the consequence, which must bewilder the scholar and appall the theologian. But such is not the case. Both do their utmost to put these remarks in some kind of order, to simplify them, to compress them into some specific idea. Maniacs of rigor, they try to find out what their author thought about eternity and death. What he thought? *Anything*. They are experiences of his, personal and absolute. As for his god, never *completed*, always imperfect and changing, Angelus Silesius registers his moments and translates his becoming into a thought which is no less imperfect and changing. Let us beware of the definitive, let us avoid those who claim to possess an exact view of anything. To be surprised that Angelus Silesius in one distich should identify death with evil, and in another with good, is to lack both probity and humor. Since death itself is a *becoming* in us, let us consider its stages, its metamorphoses; to reduce it to a formula is to halt, to impoverish, to sabotage death.

The mystic experiences neither his ecstasies nor his disgusts within the limits of a definition: his claim is not to satisfy the demands of his thought, but those of his sensations. And he tends much more toward sensation than the poet, for it is by sensation that he verges upon God.

No *frissons* are identical, none may be repeated *ad libitum*: the identity of a word conceals, as a matter of fact, a number of divergent experiences. There are a thousand perceptions of Nothing, and only one word to translate them: the indigence of language renders the universe intelligible . . . In Angelus Silesius, the interval which separates one distich from another is diminished, if not canceled, by the familiar image of the same words which recur, by that poverty of language which makes his sighs and his horrors and his ecstasies lose their individuality. Hence the mystic denatures his experience by expressing it, almost as much as the scholar denatures the mystic by glossing him.

*

It is a mistake to suppose that mysticism derives from a softening of the instincts, from a compromised vitality. A Luis of León, a John of the Cross crowned an age of great enterprises and were necessarily contemporaries of the Conquest.

Far from being defectives, they fought for their faith, attacked God head on, appropriated heaven for themselves. Their idolatry of the will's abeyance, of gentleness and passivity, secured them against a scarcely bearable tension, against that *superabundant* hysteria which is responsible for their intolerance, their proselytism, their power over this world and the next. To get a sense of them, imagine a Hernando Cortez in the middle of an invisible geography.

The German mystics were conquerors too. Their penchant for heresy, for personal assertion, for protest expressed—on the spiritual level—the will of an entire nation to individualize itself. Such was the meaning of the Reformation which gave Germany its historical orientation. At the height of the Middle Ages, Eckhart overflows the tradition and follows his own path: his vitality anticipates Luther's. He also suggests the direction German thought will take. But what assures him a unique position is that as the father of paradox in religious matters, he was the first to have given a tonality of intellectual drama to the relations between man and God. This tension was particularly appropriate to an age in which a whole people was in ferment and in search of itself.

There was something of the knight, the *Ritter*, in these mystics. Wearing a secret cuirass, invincible even in their passion for torturing themselves, they could moan with a swagger and possessed a contagious, incendiary madness.

Suso yields nothing to the most extravagant anchorites, so skillful is he in varying his torments. The knightly spirit, turned toward the intemporal, perpetuates there the love of adventures. For mysticism is an adventure, a vertical adventure: it forays upward and seizes another form of space. Thereby it differs from those doctrines of the decadence, whose characteristic is *not* to well up from the spot, to come from *elsewhere*, like those transplanted from the Orient to Rome. Hence they answered only to the thirst for stagnation of a civilization incapable of creating a new religion or of cleaving still to the glamors of mythology. The same is true of today's mystics, with their *imported* absolute, for the use of the weak and the disappointed.

Piety, that insolent sigh of the creature, is inseparable from energy and from vigor. Port-Royal, for all its idyllic appearance, was the expression of an exultant spirituality. There France knew her last moment of *interiority*. Subsequently she could lay claim to excess and power only in the lay world: she made the Revolution; after the advent of a sugared Catholicism, it was all she could undertake. Having lost the temptation of heresy, she became sterile in religious inspiration.

Refractory by vocation, rampant in their prayers, the mystics play with heaven, *trembling the while*. The Church has degraded them to the rank of supernatural mendicants so that, wretchedly civilized, they might serve as "models." Yet we know that both in their lives and in their writings they were phenomena of nature and that no worse disaster could happen to them than to fall into the hands of the priests. Our duty is to wrest them away: only at this price could Christianity still admit even a hint of duration.

When I call them "phenomena of nature," I am not claiming that their "health" was foolproof. We know that they were sick. But disease acted upon them like a goad, like a factor of excess. By sickness, they aimed at another genre of vitality than ours. Peter of Alcantara managed to sleep no more than one hour a night: was this not a sign of strength? And they were all strong, for they destroyed their bodies only in order to derive a further power from them. We think of them as gentle; no beings were tougher. What is it they propose? *The virtues of disequilibrium*. Avid for every kind of wound, hypnotized by the unwonted, they have undertaken the conquest of the only fiction worth the trouble; God owes them everything: his glory, his mystery, his eternity. They lend existence to the inconceivable, violate Nothing in order to animate it: how could gentleness accomplish such an exploit?

Contrary to that abstract, false void of the philosophers, the mystics' nothingness glistens with plenitude: delight out of this world, discharge of duration, a luminous annihilation beyond the limits of thought. To deify oneself, to destroy in order to regain oneself, to engulf oneself in one's own lucidity demands more resource and temerity than all the rest of our actions. Ecstasy—the limit-condition of sensation, fulfillment *by the wreck of consciousness*—is available only to those who, venturing outside themselves, substitute for the commonplace illusion which grounded their life another and supreme illusion in which everything is resolved, in which everything is transcended. Here the mind is suspended, reflection abolished and, with it, the logic of disarray. If we could, after the example of the mystics, pass beyond the evidence, beyond the impasse which proceeds from it, if we could become that dazzled, divine errantry, if we could, like them, reascend to the *true* nothingness! With what skill they plagiarize God, pillage Him, strip Him of His attributes with which they arm themselves in order to . . . remake Him! Nothing can resist the effervescence of their madness, that expansion of their soul forever threatening to fabricate another heaven, another earth. Everything they touch takes on the color of being. Having understood the disadvantage of seeing and of leaving things as they are, they have forced themselves to denature them. An optical defect on which they lavish all their care. No trace of reality, they know, subsists after the passage, after the devastations of clairvoyance. *Nothing is*, that is their point of departure, that is the evidence which they have managed to conquer, to reject, in order to reach the affirmation: *everything is*. Until we have followed the path which has led them to so surprising a conclusion, we shall never be on an equal footing with them.

*

Even in the Middle Ages, certain minds, tired of sifting the same themes, the same expressions, were obliged, in order to renew their piety and to emancipate it from the official terminology, to fall back on paradox, on the alluring, sometimes brutal, sometimes subtle formula. Hence Meister Eckhart. However rigorous, and however preoccupied with coherence, he was too much a writer not to seem suspect to Theology: his style, rather than his ideas, gained him the honor of being convicted of heresy. When we consider, in his treatises and sermons, the propositions condemned, we are amazed at the concern they betray for the niceties of expression; they reveal the inspired aspect of his faith. Like every heretic, he sinned on the side of form. An enemy of language, all orthodoxy, whether religious or political, postulates *the usual expression*. If almost all the mystics had their contentions with the Church, it is because they had too much talent; the Church demands none, and insists only on obedience, submission to its *style*. In the name of a sclerotic Word, the stakes, the pyres were erected. In order to escape them, the heretic had no other recourse than to change his formulas, to express his opinions in other terms, in terms that were *consecrated*. The Inquisition might never have existed if Catholicism had shown more indulgence and comprehension of the life of language, its departures, its variety, and its invention. When paradox is banned, one avoids martyrdom only by silence or banality.

Other reasons combine to make the mystic a heretic. If he is reluctant to let an external authority regulate his relations with God, he is no readier to admit meddling from on high: it is all he can do to tolerate Jesus. Anything but accommodating, he must nonetheless submit to certain compromises, mumble the recommended, the prescribed prayers, lacking the power to improvise ever-fresh ones. Let us forgive him this weakness. Perhaps he stoops to it only to prove that he is capable of lowering himself to the level of the vulgar and of employing their language; perhaps, too, to prove that he is not ignorant of the temptation of humility. But we know that he does not yield to it often, that he loves to innovate when he prays, that he invents on his knees, and that this is his way of breaking with the God of the common.

The mystic reanimates and rehabilitates faith, threatens and undermines it as an intimate, providential enemy. Without him, it would wither. We can guess now the reason why Christianity is dying and why the Church, deprived of both apologists and detractors, no longer thrives on praise or persecution. Fresh out of heretics, she would gladly stop demanding obedience if, in return, she discerned among her own a single fanatic who, deigning to attack her, to take her seriously, might give her some hope, some reason for alarm. To shelter so many idols and to glimpse not one iconoclast on the horizon! The faithful no longer vie with each other, nor the unbelievers, moreover: no one tries to come in first in the race for salvation or damnation . . .

A considerable occurrence: the two greatest modern poets, Shakespeare and Hölderlin, have *bypassed* Christianity. If they had yielded to its seduction, they would have made their own mythology out of it, and the Church would have had the luck of counting in her ranks two more heresiarchs. Without deigning to attack the Cross, still less to pull it up to their own level, one passed beyond it to the gods, the other resuscitated those of Greece. The first rose above prayer, the second invoked a heaven which he knew to be impotent, which he loved *defunct:* one is the precursor of our indifference, the other of our regrets.

*

The solitary, in his own way a combatant, feels the need to populate his solitude with enemies, whether real or imaginary. If he believes, he fills it with demons, as to whose reality he allows himself no illusion. Without them, he would fall into insipidity: his spiritual life would suffer. It was appropriately that Jakob Boehme called the Devil "Nature's cook," whose art lends a savor to everything. God himself, positing from the first the necessity of the adversary, acknowledged that He could not do without a struggle, attacking and being attacked.

As the mystic, in most cases, invents his adversaries, it follows that his thought asserts the existence of others by calculation, by artifice: it is a strategy of no consequence. His thought boils down, in the last instance, to a polemic with himself: he seeks to be, he becomes a crowd, even if it is only by making himself one new mask after the other, multiplying his faces: in which he resembles his Creator, whose histrionics he perpetuates.

*

The mystical phenomenon lacks continuity: it flourishes, achieves its apogee, then degenerates and ends in a caricature. Such was the case of the religious flowering in Spain, in the Low Countries or in Germany. If, in the arts, the epigone manages to inspire respect, nothing is more pathetic, on the other hand, than a second-class mystic, parasite of the sublime, plagiarist of ecstasies. One can play at poetry, one can even give the illusion of originality: it suffices to have penetrated the secrets of the trade. These secrets count for nothing in the eyes of the mystic, whose art is only a *means.* Since he does not aspire to please men and seeks to be read *elsewhere,* he addresses himself to a rather limited public, a rather difficult audience which demands of him much more than talent or genius. What does he work for? To find what escapes or survives the disintegration of his experiences: the residue of intemporality under the ego's vibrations. He erodes his senses in contact with the indestructible, contrary to the poet who exhausts *his* in contact with the provisional; one wrecks himself almost carnally in the Supreme (mysticism: *the physiology of essences*), the other revels on the surface of himself. Two sensualists, at different levels. Having once tasted appearances, the poet cannot forget their savor; it is the mystic who, unable to rise to the voluptuous pleasure of silence, restricts himself to that of the word. A chatterbox of quality, a *superior* soliloquist.

*

When we read the Revelations of Margaret Ebner, when we follow her through her *crises* into her adorable hell, we are filled with . . . jealousy. For days at a time she could not unclench her teeth; when finally she opened her mouth, it was to utter cries which exalted and terrorized the convent. And what can we say about Angela of Foligno? Let us listen to her instead: "I contemplate, in the abyss into ./hich I see I have fallen, the glut of my iniquities, I seek, to no avail, how to discover and manifest them to the world, I would walk naked through cities and squares, meat and fishes hung from my neck and crying out: here is the vile creature!"

Sanguine temperaments, delighting in the extremity of degradation and of purity, in the delirum of the depths and of the heights, the saints do not accommodate themselves to our rationalizations, nor to our cowardices. To see them as meditative souls is to deceive oneself altogether. Too unbridled, too fierce to be able to stop at meditation (which supposes self-control and hence a mediocrity of the blood), if they aspire to descend to the foundations of things, the steps that lead them there are not precisely "reflective." Without prudence, without the least trace of stoicism in their gestures and their words, they believe everything is permitted to them, they parade their indiscretion through the hearts they trouble because they abominate peace and cannot endure a soul that has *arrived*. Indeed they would damn rather than accept themselves. Listen to Angela of Foligno once again: "Should all the sages of the world and all the saints of Paradise shower me with their consolations and their promises, and God Himself with His gifts, if He did not change me from such as I am, if He did not begin a new work in the depths of my soul instead of giving me ease, then the sages, the saints and God would exasperate beyond all expression my despair, my rage, my melancholy and my blindness." Must we not, in the face of such declarations and such demands, liquidate our last vestiges of good sense and fling ourselves, like barbarians, toward the "darkness of the light"? Yet how can we bring ourselves to do it, fastened as we are to the infirmities of modesty? Our blood is too tepid, our appetites too well trained. No chance of getting *beyond* ourselves. Even our madness is too measured. To knock down the partitions of the mind, to shake it up, to seek its ruin—wellspring of the new! As it is, the mind is refractory to the invisible and perceives only what it already knows. To open itself to the true learning, it must be dislocated, must exceed its bounds, must pass through orgies of annihilation. Ignorance would not be our fate if we dared hoist ourselves above our certitudes and above that timidity which, keeping us from working miracles, bogs us down in ourselves. O for the pride of the saints!

If they keep their vigils and pray, it is to tap the secret of God's power. Perfidious supplications, the prayers of these rebels around whom the Demon prowls by choice. Cunning, they tap his secret, too, and force him to work for them. The wicked principle which inhabits them they know how to use—in order to *ascend*. Those among them who break down do so with a certain complacency: they collapse not as victims but as colleagues of the Devil. Saved or lost, all bear a mark of non-humanity, all scorn to assign a limit to their undertakings. If they renounce, their renunciation is complete. But instead of being diminished and weakened thereby, they find themselves more powerful than the rest of us, who preserve what they have abandoned. These giants with their shattered bodies and souls—terrify us. Contemplating them, we are ashamed of being men and nothing more. And if, in their turn, they contemplate us, we decipher the words with which our mediocrity inspires their mercy: "Poor creatures who lack the courage to become unique, to become monsters." Decidedly, the Devil labors for them and is no stranger to their aureole. What a humiliation for the rest of us, to have come to terms with him for nothing!

*

A destructor in the service of life, a demon *oriented to good*, the saint is the grand master of the effort against the ego. To vanquish his tendencies as much as in terror of himself, he keeps on a regimen of goodness and, supposing himself to have brothers and duties toward them, imposes on himself the overwork of pity. He suffers, and loves to suffer, but at the end of his sufferings, he makes beings into his playthings, rushes into the future, reads the thoughts of others, heals the incurable, infringes the laws of nature with impunity. It is to acquire this freedom and this power that he has prayed and resisted temptations. Pleasure, as he is aware, relaxes, softens: if he were to resort to it, he could no longer accede nor even aspire to the extraordinary, his strength and his faculties would diminish: no longer any energy in his desires nor any flexibility in his ambition. What he seeks are satisfactions of another order, and a kind of exemplary voluptuousness: that of equaling God. His horror of the senses is calculated, and anything but disinterested.

He persecutes and rejects them, knowing he will rediscover them, transfigured, elsewhere.

The moment he aspires to substitute himself for the divinity, the saint agrees to pay the price: so great an end justifies any and every means. Convinced that eternity is the apanage of a dilapidated body, he will seek out all kinds of infirmities and conspire against his well-being, from whose ruin he will expect his salvation and his triumph. If he let himself follow his own nature, he would perish; but since he utilizes his mistreated vitality, he recovers. Too long contained, it explodes. And he becomes a fearful invalid who turns toward heaven in order to dislodge the usurper there. Such a favor, dispensed to those who, by suffering, have penetrated the secret of Creation, is met with only in periods when sanctity is identified with disgrace.

*

Every inspired state proceeds from a cultivated, willed inanition. Sanctity—uninterrupted inspiration—is an art of letting oneself die of hunger without . . . dying, a challenge hurled at one's entrails, and a kind of demonstration of the incompatibility of ecstasy and digestion. A well-fed humanity produces skeptics, never saints. The absolute? A matter of diet. No "inner fire," no "flame" without the virtually complete suppression of nourishment. Let us counter our appetites: our organs will burn, our substance catch fire. He who eats his fill is spiritually doomed.

Moved by savage impulses, the saints had managed to master them, hence to preserve them in secret. They were aware that charity derives its power from our physiological dramas, and that in order to attach themselves to beings they must declare war on the body, pervert it, martyr it, and subjugate it. Each of them evokes an aggressor who, suddenly converted to love, would subsequently employ himself in hating himself. And they knew how to hate themselves to the very end; but, since this self-hatred was exhausted, they were free, released from all shackles: the *askesis* had revealed to them the meaning, the usefulness of destruction, prelude to purity and deliverance. In their turn, they will reveal to us what pangs we must suffer if we, too, seek to be free.

At whatever level our life is lived, it will be truly our own only in proportion to our efforts to break its apparent forms. Ennui, despair, *abulia* itself will aid us here, on condition, of course, that we make our experience of them complete, that we live them through to the moment when, risking surrender, we rise up and transform them into auxiliaries of our vitality. What is more fruitful than the worst, for the man who knows how to *desire* it? For it is not suffering which liberates, but the desire to suffer.

*

How can we laugh at the hysteria of the Middle Ages? In your cell you sighed or shrieked: the others venerated you . . . Your troubles did not lead you to the psychiatrist. Lest you be cured of them, you exasperated them, while you concealed your health like a stigma, a vice. Disease was the general recourse, the great remedy. Nowadays, fallen into discredit, boycotted, it continues to reign, but no one loves it, no one seeks it out. Sick men, we are at a loss for what to do with our ills. More than one of our madnesses will remain forever unexploited.

There are other hysterias which are no less admirable, those which generate hymns to the Sun, to Being, to the Unknown. Dawn of Egypt, of Greece, frenzy of mythologies, accents in first contact with the elements! At their antipodes, we are unfit to thrill to the spectacle of origins: our interrogations, instead of leaping in rhythms, drag in the lees of concept or are disfigured beneath the sneer of our systems. Where is our hymnic sensibility, the intoxication of our beginnings, the dawn of our stupefactions? Let us fling ourselves at the Pythoness' feet, returning to our old ecstasies: the philosophy of *unique moments,* the only philosophy . . .

*

Once we have ceased linking our secret life to God, we can ascend to ecstasies as effective as those of the mystics and conquer this world without recourse to the Beyond. And if, nonetheless, the obsession of another world were to pursue us, it would be permissible to construct, to project one for the occasion, if only to satisfy our thirst for the invisible. What matters are our sensations, their intensity and their virtues, as our capacity to fling ourselves into a madness that is *not sacred.* In the unknown, we can go as far as the saints, without making use of their means. It will be enough for us to constrain reason to a long silence. Handed over to ourselves, nothing will keep us from acceding to the delicious suspension of all our faculties. A man who has glimpsed these states knows that our movements there lose their habitual direction: we ascend to the abyss, we fall into heaven. Where are we? A question without object: we no longer *take place* . . .

RAGES AND
RESIGNATIONS

THE CAREER OF WORDS

To discover, and to be convinced, that the history of ideas is no more than a parade of labels converted into so many absolutes, we need merely consider the most decisive philosophical events of the last century.

We know the triumph of "science" in the era of positivism. A man who appealed to that authority could rave on in peace: everything was allowed him once he invoked "rigor" or "experimental method." Matter and Energy made their appearance shortly afterward: the prestige of their capitals did not last long. Indiscreet, insinuating Evolution gained ground at their expense. A learned synonym of "progress," an optimistic forgery of "destiny," it claimed to eliminate all mystery and to dictate to the intelligence: a cult grew up around the word, comparable to the one dedicated to the "people." Though it has managed to survive its vogue, yet it no longer awakens any lyrical accent: exalt it and you compromise yourself or seem old-fashioned.

Toward the beginning of the century our confidence in concepts was shaken. Intuition, with its escort: duration, *élan vital, etc.*, was to profit thereby, and to prevail for a certain time. Then we needed something new: it was the turn of Existence. A magical word which excited both specialists and dilettantes. The key had been found at last. And one was no longer an individual, one was an Existent.

Who will compile a dictionary of words by epochs, an inventory of philosophic fashions? The enterprise would show us that a system dates by its terminology, that it always wears itself out by its form. Take a thinker who might interest us still—we refuse to reread him because we cannot endure the verbal apparatus which his ideas require. Borrowings from philosophy are mortal to literature. (Recall certain fragments of Novalis spoiled by the Fichtean dialect.) Doctrines die by what had insured their success: by style. For them to revive, we must rethink them in our own jargon or else imagine them before their elaboration, in their original and formless reality.

Among the important words, there is one whose career, a particularly long one, provokes melancholy reflections. I have named the Soul. When we consider its present state, its pitiable end, we are nonplussed. Yet it had *begun* well. Recall the rank Neoplatonism assigned it: a cosmic principle a derivative of the intelligible world. All the ancient doctrines stamped with mysticism were based on it. Less concerned to define its nature than to determine its use for the believer, Christianity reduced it to human dimensions. How it must have regretted the days when it embraced nature and enjoyed the privilege of being at once an immense reality and an explanatory principle! In the modern world, the Soul managed to regain some territory, little by little, and to consolidate its positions. Believers and unbelievers were to take it into account, preserve it, even presume on it; if only to oppose it, the Soul was still cited even in the palmy days of materialism; and philosophers, so reticent in its regard, nonetheless reserved a corner for it in their systems.

Today, who bothers about it? The Soul is mentioned only

inadvertently; its place is in songs: melody alone makes it endurable, makes us forget its decrepitude. Discourse no longer tolerates it: having assumed too many meanings, and served too many uses, it has frayed, deteriorated, fallen. Its patron, the psychologist, by constantly patching it up, was to finish it off. Hence it now awakens in our conscience only that regret associated with the kind of success forever a thing of the past. And to think that once the sages venerated it, set it above the gods, and sacrificed the universe to it!

SOCRATES

Had he specified the nature of his daemon, he would have spoiled a good deal of his glory. His discretion in the matter inspired as much curiosity among his contemporaries as it does today; it also permits historians of philosophy to haggle over a case in every way alien to their preoccupations. This case reminds us of another—Pascal's abyss. For philosophy, two tempting weaknesses, or two pirouettes . . . The abyss in question, of course, is less disconcerting. For a mind openly at war with reason, what could be more natural than to acknowledge—and appropriate—an abyss? But was it as natural that the inventor of the concept, the promoter of rationalism, should act on the authority of "inner voices"?

Ambiguity of this kind is unfailingly fertile for the thinker who intends to reach posterity. We never follow the consistent rationalist for long; once we pluck out his mystery and know where he is headed, we abandon him to his system. Both calculating and inspired, Socrates gave his contradictions just the nuance that would bewilder and baffle us. Was his daemon purely a psychological phenomenon or did it correspond to a metaphysical reality? Was it of divine origin or did it answer only an ethical purpose? Did he really hear it or was it only a hallucination? Hegel calls it a subjective oracle with no external reality; Nietzsche dismisses it as an actor's trick.

Yet how can you play the part of the-man-who-hears-voices all your life? If not impossible, sustaining such a role would be a difficult task, even for a Socrates. Actually it is of little consequence whether he was dominated by his daemon or merely *used* it in the service of the cause! If he made it up out of whole cloth, he must have been obliged to, if only to protect himself from others. A solitary hemmed in by society, his first duty was to escape his entourage by taking refuge in mystery, whether authentic or equivocal. How distinguish between the real daemon and the spurious one, between a secret and the appearance of a secret? How determine whether Socrates was waylaying, or only wandering?

The fact remains that if his teaching leaves us indifferent, the argument he provoked about himself still affects us: he was the first thinker to make himself into a *case*, and it is with him that the inextricable problem of sincerity begins.

EPICURUS

When the problem of happiness supplants that of knowledge, philosophy abandons its proper domain to engage in a suspect activity: it concerns itself with man . . . Questions it would once have scorned asking now attract its attention, and it attempts to answer them in all seriousness. "How is suffering to be avoided?" is the first to entice it. In a phase of lassitude, increasingly alien to impersonal concerns, to the thirst for knowledge, it abandons speculation and to the truths that disturb prefers those that console.

It was such truths that a sick and enslaved Greece sought from Epicurus: a recipe for rest, a remedy for anxiety. He was to his age what the psychoanalyst is to ours: in his way, did he too not expose "civilization and its discontents?" (In every chaotic and over-refined age, a Freud attempts to disencumber men's souls.) Even more than Socrates, it is Epicurus who nudged Philosophy toward Therapeutics. To cure, above all to cure oneself—such was his ambition: though he wished to free men from fear of death and fear of the gods, he himself suffered from both. The *ataraxia* he prided himself on was not his usual experience: his "sensibility" was notorious. As for his scorn of the sciences, for which he was later to be reproached, we know it is often the characteristic of "tender hearts." This theoretician of happiness was a sick man; apparently he had vomiting fits twice a day. With what suffering he had to contend for having so hated "the sickness of the soul!" The little serenity he managed to acquire he doubtless reserved for his disciples; grateful and naive, they gave him a reputation for wisdom. Since our illusions are much weaker than those of his contemporaries, we have no trouble seeing his Garden as the compost heap it was.

SAINT PAUL

We can never punish him enough for making Christianity impolite, for saddling it with the nastiest traditions of the Old Testament: intolerance, brutality, provincialism. How indiscreetly he meddles in matters which are none of his business and of which he has no understanding at all. His remarks on virginity, abstinence, and marriage are nothing short of disgusting. Accountable for our religious and ethical prejudices, he has determined the norms of our stupidity and multiplied those restrictions which still paralyze our instincts.

With none of the prophets' lyricism, none of their cosmic and elegiac accents, Paul echoes only their sectarianism, their lapses into bad taste, verbiage, and marketplace rant. It is *mores* that interest him. Once he gets on the subject, his voice cracks with malice. As much obsessed by the City he would destroy as by the one he would build, he pays less attention to relations between man and God than to those between man and man. Read the famous Epistles carefully:

not one moment of detachment or delicacy or distinction; everything is breathless frenzy, plebeian hysteria, hatred of learning and of the solitude which is its condition. Intermediaries everywhere, connections, contacts, clannishness: the Father, the Mother, the Son, angels, saints—not a trace of intellectuality, no coherence of concept, no attempt to *understand*. Sins, retributions, the bookkeeping of vice and virtue. A religion without inquiry: an anthropomorphic debauch. I blush for the God it offers; disqualifying Him constitutes a duty.

Neither Lao-Tse nor Buddha allude to an identifiable Being; scorning the artifices of faith, they invite us to meditation; to engage our minds, they establish its limit: the Tao, Nirvana. They had a different notion of man.

How meditate if everything must be referred to a supreme . . . individual? What can we seek with psalms and prayers? What can we find? It is out of sloth that we personify our divinity and then appeal to Him. The Greeks awakened to philosophy the moment their gods were no longer adequate; ideas begin where Olympus leaves off. To think is to stop venerating, to rebel against the enigma and proclaim its bankruptcy.

*

By adopting a doctrine originally alien to him, the convert imagines he has taken a step toward himself, when he has merely sidestepped his problems. To escape insecurity —his ruling passion—he pledges himself to the first cause chance affords. Once in possession of the "Truth" he will revenge himself on others for his old uncertainties, his old fears. This was the case of Saint Paul, the arch-convert. His grandiloquence betrays an anxiety he will make every effort to dispel, without success.

Like all neophytes, he thought his new faith would transform his nature and triumph over those hesitations he was so careful to keep from his correspondents and his listeners. His tricks no longer take us in, but in the past many minds permitted themselves to be duped. Granted, that was when we sought the "truth," when we were not yet interested in *cases.* If our apostle was badly received in Athens, if he found there a society contemptuous of his lucubrations, it is because in Athens men were still *arguing,* because skepticism, far from abandoning, still defended its positions. In Athens, the Christian gibberish could get nowhere; on the other hand, it was to seduce Corinth, a vulgar city inimical to dialectic.

The mob asks to be overwhelmed by invective, by threats and revelations, by shattering pronouncements: the mob loves a shouter. Paul was one, the most inspired, the most talented, the most artful of antiquity. We still can hear the echoes of the noise he made. He knew how to hoist himself onto the stage and, once there, how to hold it. He was the first barker of the Greco-Roman world. The sages of his time recommended silence, resignation, withdrawal—impractical things; shrewder, Paul came along with his alluring recipes: the ones that redeem the riffraff and demoralize the refined. His revenge upon Athens was complete. Had he been more successful there, his spleen might have been less. And if we are mutilated pagans, pilloried, crucified, susceptible to profound vulgarity, we have this failure to thank for it.

*

A gentile Jew, a perverted Jew, a traitor. Which accounts for the odor of insincerity that clings to his appeals, his exhortations, his violence. He is suspect: he sounds too *convinced.* One never knows where to get hold of him, how to define him; standing at an intersection of history, he is subject to many influences. After hesitating among several roads, he finally chooses one—*the way.* Men of his stamp play for high stakes: obsessed by posterity, by the echoes their actions will raise, if they sacrifice themselves to a cause, it is as *effective* victims.

Whenever I am at a loss for a scapegoat I open the Epistles and am quickly reassured. I have my man, and he rouses me to a fury. To hate him *up close*, as a contemporary, I cancel out twenty centuries and follow him on his rounds; his successes discourage me, his tortures fill me with delight. The frenzy he communicates I turn against him: unfortunately, the Empire proceeded otherwise.

A decadent civilization compromises with its disease, cherishes the virus infecting it, loses its self-respect, permits a Paul to circulate . . . By the same token, it admits defeat, worm-eaten, done for. The smell of carrion fascinates and inflames those greedy and garrulous gravediggers we call the Apostles.

A world of magnificence and light fell before these "enemies of the Muses," these fierce invaders who even today affect us with a certain dread—tempered by a certain distaste. Paganism regarded them with irony, a harmless weapon too noble to reduce a horde indifferent to nuance. The man of discernment who reasons cannot measure himself against the Boeotian who prays. Frozen in the high altitudes of sarcasm and satire, he will succumb to the first assault, for energy, privilege of the dregs, always comes from below.

Antiquity's horrors were infinitely preferable to those of Christianity. These frenzied minds, these souls riven by irrelevant remorse, these wreckers roused against the amenities cherished by a senile society, were to abuse understanding by turning it into "heart." The ablest among them fell to his task with a perversity which at first scandalized but ultimately scarred, scored and secured allegiance to an unmentionable cause.

Yet the Greco-Roman twilight deserved another enemy, another promise, another religion. What grounds for granting even a grain of human progress when we think how easily the Christian fables snuffed out stoicism! If the latter had managed to propagate, take possession of the world, men might have *come to something*, or almost. Resignation, had it become compulsory, would have taught us to endure our misfortunes with dignity, to contemplate our nullity in silence. Would poetry have evaporated from our world? So much the worse for poetry! In exchange, we should have captured the faculty of suffering our destinies without a murmur: accusing no one, condescending to neither melancholy nor mirth nor regret, reducing our relations with the universe to a harmonious system of defeats, living as condemned men may live—not imploring divinity but offering it a warning . . . It could never be. Overrun on every side, stoicism, faithful to its principles, had the elegance to die without a struggle. A religion erects itself on the ruins of wisdom: the latter's strategy is hardly suitable to the former. When they must despair, men will always prefer kneeling to standing. It is their cowardice, their fatigue that aspires to salvation, their incapacity to embrace comfortlessness and in it find the justification of pride. Shame on the man who dies escorted to his grave by the miserable hopes that have kept him alive. Let the mob and its mouthpieces crawl into the "ideal" and be swallowed up. Solitude is a mission, not a *donnée*; to rise to its level and assume it means renouncing the vulgarity that insures success, religious or otherwise. Recapitulate the history of ideas, acts, attitudes and you find that the *future* was always on the side of the rabble. One does not preach in the name of Marcus Aurelius: since he spoke only to himself, he had neither disciples nor votaries; on the other hand, temples are still being built where certain Epistles are cited to satiety. As long as this goes on, I shall persecute this saint so adept at interesting us in his torments.

LUTHER

To have faith is not everything—not even enough; you must also endure it like a curse, seeing in God an enemy, an executioner, an ogre, yet loving Him nevertheless, assigning Him all the inhumanity you can muster, can imagine . . . The Church turns Him into an easygoing figure of fun; Luther protests: God, he declares, is neither the "simpleton," the "meek spirit" nor the "cuckold" proposed to our veneration, but a "devouring fire," a fury "more terrible than the Devil," who loves to torment us. Not that Luther is in any way intimidated by God. On occasion he berates Him, treating Him as his peer: "If God fails to protect me and to save my honor, the shame will be His." He knows how to kneel, to humble himself, but he also knows how to be insolent, to supplicate in the tones of provocation, to shift from sighs to reproaches, to pray in *polemics*. For him any term will serve to worship or to curse, even the coarsest. Calling God to order, Luther has given a new meaning to humility, setting up an exchange between the miseries of the Creator and those of His creatures. An end to piety, and to emasculated doubt. Even a minimum of aggressiveness is enough to reawaken faith: God ignores mealy-mouthed appeals; He prefers to be summoned, jostled, enjoying with His own those very misunderstandings the Church exerts itself to dispel. The Church, monitoring the *style* of its flock, intercepts Heaven, which reacts only to imprecations, to abuse, to expressions defying the censorship of theology or good taste, or even the control of . . . reason itself.

As for what reason is worth, don't ask the philosophers, for it is their job to flatter and protect it. To penetrate its arcana, turn instead to those who know reason to their cost and in the flesh. It is not an accident that Luther calls reason a whore. By nature and function, reason is a whore, surviving by simulation, versatility, and shamelessness. Stopping at nothing, since it *is* nothing, reason gives itself to each man, and each man may claim it as his own: the just and the unjust, the martyr and the tyrant. There is no cause reason does not serve, putting all on the same plane, without reticence, without predilection; the first-comer obtains its favors as the last. Only the naive still proclaim it our greatest possession. Luther has exposed it for what it is. Of course, not everyone has been granted the privilege of a visit from the Devil.

*

Minds that hurl themselves into temptation, living on intimate terms with the Evil One, fleeing him only to find him . . . "I wore him," Luther says, "hanging around my neck, he slept beside me, in my bed, more often than my wife." He even reaches the point of wondering "if perhaps the Devil is not God."

Far from being a haven, Luther's faith was a self-induced shipwreck, eagerly sought after, a danger which flattered and exalted him in his own eyes. Pure, religion would be sterile; what is profound and virulent in it is not the divine but the demoniacal. And the attempt to spare it the Devil's society would render it anemic and mawkish, would degrade it. To believe in the reality of salvation you must first believe in the reality of the Fall: every religious act begins with the perception of hell—the raw material of faith— heaven comes only *afterwards*, a kind of corrective, a consolation: a luxury, a superfetation, an accident required by our bias in favor of symmetry and balance. Only the Devil is *necessary*. The religion that dispenses with the Enemy debilitates itself, grows sterile, becomes a vague, querulous piety. The man who seeks salvation at any cost will never have much of a religious career.

The virtue of the Reformation was to have troubled Europe's sleep, rejecting the Roman tranquilizers and opposing the image of a benevolent God and a mediocre Satan with that of an equivocal divinity and an omnipotent Devil. As Luther knew, the concept of predestination is profoundly immoral. All the more reason for him to support and promote it. His mission was to shock, to scandalize the mind, aggravate its pangs and drive it to impossible hopes—in a word, to *reduce the number of the elect*. He had the honesty to admit that on certain points he yielded to the Adversary's suggestions. Which accounts for his temerity in condemning the majority of believers. Was he trying to disconcert? Undoubtedly. The cynicism of prophets reconciles us to their doctrines, and even to their victims . . .

*

Despite his incapacity to hope, Luther nevertheless personifies the emancipator; more than one liberal movement derives directly from him. This is because he proclaims God's absolute sovereignty only to abase any other form of authority. "To be a prince," he says, "and not be a pirate is almost impossible." Fine as the maxims of sedition are, those of heresy are finer still. If Europe can be construed as a succession of schisms, if its glories are nothing but a train of heterodoxies, it is Luther we have to thank for it. Ancestor of scores of innovators, he nevertheless had the advantage over them of not yielding to optimism, the vice that dishonors so many revolutions. Closer than we are to the sources of Sin, he could not avoid the fact that to free a man does not necessarily mean to save him.

*

Tossed back and forth between the Middle Ages and the Renaissance, torn by contradictory impulses and convictions, this Rabelais of *angst* was the ideal man to breathe new life into a fainting, fading Christianity. Only Luther knew what measures to take to deepen its colors: his piety was *black.* Even Pascal's, even Kierkegaard's pale beside his: the former too much a writer, the latter too much a philosopher. But Luther, with the strength of his peasant neurasthenia, possessed the instinct necessary to collar both the forces of Good and those of Evil. Unceremonious, savory, his coarseness is never offensive. There is nothing false about him, nothing of the classic apostle: neither scholarly hatred nor studied vehemence. In the off-handedness of his terrors sounds a note of humor: precisely what was lacking among the promoters of the Cross. Luther? A humanized Paul.

ORIGINS

After having assumed the insomnia of the sap and the blood, the panic which traverses the animate, must we not return to somnolence and to the non-knowledge of our earliest solitudes? And while a world anterior to our waking solicits us, we envy the indifference, the perfect apoplexy of the mineral, free of the tribulations that lie in wait for the living, for all condemned souls. Sure of itself, the stone claims nothing, whereas the tree, that mute entreaty, and the animal, an agonizing appeal, torment themselves this side of speech. Ages of silence and of screams wait in vain for us to deliver them, to serve as their interpreters; deserters of the word, we no longer aspire to anything but the reign of the undifferentiated, the darkness and the drunkenness of an epoch before daybreak, the uninterrupted ecstasy at the heart of that original opacity whose traces, now and then, we rediscover deep in ourselves or on the periphery of God.

BEYOND SELF-PITY

Do not confuse a man who pities himself with a man who is defeated: he still possesses energy enough to protect himself against the dangers which threaten him. Let him complain! That is his way of disguising his vitality. He asserts himself as best he can: his tears often conceal an aggressive intention.

Nor must you take his lyricism or his cynicism for signs of weakness; lyricism and cynicism emanate from a latent strength, from a capacity to expand or refuse. Depending on circumstances, he employs one or the other: he is well armed. Furthermore, he enjoys the consolations of an existence without a horizon, an existence appeased, imbued with its impasses, proud of culminating in a defeat. Leave him, then, to his felicity. On the other hand, mind the man who can no longer pity himself, who rejects his miseries, relegates them outside his nature and outside his voice. Having renounced the resources of lamentation and derision, he ceases to communicate with his life which he turns into an object. His very sufferings supervene apart from his ego, and if he records them it is to debase them, to make them into *things*, to abandon them to matter. No one, not even himself, knows what he still reacts to. Disconcerted, the wise turn from him; but perhaps he will arouse the pity or jealousy of the mad, if they could realize that he, without losing his reason, has gone further than they.

PLEASURES OF THE ABYSS

That intolerance of any solution, any attempt to end the course of knowledge, that aversion for the definitive—when the believer experiences *them*, he thinks only of punishing himself for having yielded to the lures of salvation. Thus he invents sin, or turns to his own "darkness" which, too effective to be merely invented, seizes on his faith, unsettles it and makes it a flaw in the Light.

I cannot keep from reading certain religious thinkers, from wallowing in their dismay, from ravening on it. I attend, delighted, the terrors of a Pascal, and marvel at how much he is one of us. Romanticism has merely diluted his themes: Sénancour is a diffuse Pascal, Chateaubriand a sonorous Pascal. Among the motifs of recent psychology, there are few which Pascal has not touched on or anticipated. But he has done better than that: by stuffing religion with doubts and by identifying it with a deliberate stupor, he has rehabilitated it in the eyes of the unbeliever. Ambitious, aching, indiscreet in his way, this scandal-monger of heaven and hell must have envied the saints and suffered the vexation of not equaling them, of having only a lacerated faith to face them with: O happy raggedness, without which he would have left some insipid *Fioretti* or some soporific *Introduction à la vie dévote.*

Boredom, the ennui which preoccupied him a little more than Grace, he ponders incessantly, making it our substance, the "venom" of our mind, the principle which resides "in the depths of the heart." Do some say he merely pretends to suffer from it? Nothing could be more untrue; we can play at charity or piety, pray by persuasion (as he did), clasp our hands and assume the requisite posture (as he recommended); but boredom—no practice, no tradition, no method disposes us to it; no doctrine champions it; no belief absolves it. It is a condemned sentiment. Pascal replied to its solicitations because he found it in himself and perhaps loved its "venom." He is haunted by it, as he is by "glory," of which he speaks with such acuity that it is difficult to believe it was more than just an excuse for him to denounce our vanity. He describes our need of it, and analyzes it in all its details; a suspect and revealing minuteness: an obsession with glory often conceals the operations of boredom . . .

Impure like every moralist, eager to bind us to our torments and somehow to our wounds, he will have taught us to hate ourselves, to savor the pangs of self-loathing; if our conscience suppurates, if we are invalids in ecstasy, fanatics of our own rottenness, the responsibility for it is his.

Disincarnate and sensual at once, when he tends our insignificance, we feel him trembling with satisfaction; our void is his vertigo; sympathetic to all that annihilates us, enthralled by the contrast of infinite with infinitesimal, he participates as a connoisseur in the spectacle of our corruption: has he not initiated an art of extracting from our diseases the substance of our delights?

Pleasures of self-loathing: comfort of the abyss! Let us no longer pity the man who discerned one at his side: in it, no doubt, he found his delight, while (to save face) he simulated terror. But the greatest minds lie to us about their pleasures, one of which is to be a voyeur of the void. To acknowledge it without a blush requires the shamelessness of recent times and that curiosity we all feel about our own secrets. Hence his soundings in the "depths of the heart" were to lead to the discovery of the Unconscious, that latest version of the Pascalian *ténèbres*.

THE FIRST STEP TOWARD DELIVERANCE

To make an essential experiment, to free oneself from appearances, it is not necessary to confront the great problems; anyone can descant on God or acquire a metaphysical shellac. Reading, conversation, leisure suffice. Nothing is more commonplace than the *ersatz* troubled soul, for everything can be learned, even *angst*.

Yet the genuine troubled soul, the *naturally* troubled soul, exists all the same. You will recognize him by the way he reacts to words. Does he discern their insolvency? does their fiasco make him first suffer, then rejoice? Then you are, no doubt about it, in the presence of a mind emancipated or about to be. Since it is words that bind us to things, we cannot detach ourselves from things unless we first break with words. The man who relies on them, even if he is a party to every wisdom, remains in servitude and ignorance. On the other hand, anyone who turns from words in horror approaches his deliverance. This horror cannot be learned or communicated: it is brewed in the deepest part of ourselves. A poor wreck who, by the collusion of his anxieties, suffers it, is closer to true knowledge, is more "liberated" than a philosopher unfit to experience it. This is because philosophy, far from eliminating the inessential, digests and delights in it: are not all the efforts it deploys meant to keep us from realizing the double nullity of the word and the world?

THE LANGUAGE OF IRONY

However close we may be to paradise, irony bars our way. "Ineptitudes—" it chides us, "your ideas of an immemorial or future felicity. Cure yourself of your nostalgias, of the childish obsession with the beginning and the end of time. Eternity, that dead duration—only the weak are concerned with such things. Let the moment do its work, let it reabsorb your dreams."

And if we turn our eyes toward knowledge? Irony shows us its inanity, its absurdity: "What is the good of degrading *things* into problems? Your learning is constantly canceling itself out, so that the latest item shows no advance whatever over the first. Confined in the *déjà su*, you have no other substance but that of words: thought does not adhere to being."

And when, dazed, we think of some Hindu monk who, for nine years, stood against a wall in paralyzed meditation, irony intervenes once more to inform us that he discovered, at the end of so many sufferings, the nothingness by which he had begun! "You see," it insinuates, "how comical the mind's adventures are. Sacrifice them for appearances. But do not seek some reality behind them, some secret: nothing has a reality or a secret. Forbear searching the illusion, forbear destroying the unique reality."

By persisting in this language, irony accustoms us to it, compromising both our metaphysical experiments and the models which invited us to make them. And when it is *darkened* by humor, irony excludes us forever from that future *outside of time* which is the absolute.

CRUELTY—A LUXURY

In normal doses, fear, indispensable to action and thought, stimulates our senses and our mind; without it, no action at all. But when it is excessive, when it invades and overwhelms us, fear is transformed into a harmful principle, into cruelty. A man who trembles dreams of making others tremble, a man who lives in terror ends his days in ferocity. Hence the case of the Roman emperors. Anticipating their own murders, they consoled themselves by massacres . . . The discovery of a first conspiracy awakened and released in them the monster. And it was into cruelty that they withdrew in order to forget fear.

But we, ordinary mortals who cannot permit ourselves the luxury of being cruel to others—it is upon ourselves, upon our flesh and our minds that we must exercise and indeed exorcise our terrors. The tyrant in us trembles; he must act, discharge his rage, take revenge; and it is upon ourselves that he does so. So decides the modesty of our condition. Amid our terrors, more than one of us evokes a Nero who, lacking an empire, would have had only his own conscience to persecute.

ANALYSIS OF THE SMILE

To discover whether or not a man is a prey to madness, you need merely observe his *smile*. Does it leave you with an impression close to discomfort? Now is your chance for some amateur psychiatry . . .

We rightly suspect the smile which does not adhere to a person, which seems to come from elsewhere, from *another*; it does come, in fact, from another, from the madman who lies in wait, preparing, organizing himself before declaring himself.

A fugitive light given off by ourselves, our smile lasts as long as it should, without extending beyond the occasion or the pretext which has provoked it. Since it does not linger upon our countenance, it is difficult to notice: it cleaves to a given situation, it is exhausted in the moment. The other smile, the suspect one, survives the event which gave it birth, lingers, perpetuates itself, cannot disappear. At first it solicits our attention, intrigues us, then vexes, disturbs, and obsesses us. Try as we will to discount or reject it, it *regards* us, and we regard it. No way of eluding it, of protecting ourselves against its power of insinuation. The impression of *malaise* it first inspired in us swells, deepens, and turns to terror. But the smile, unable to end, spreads as though detached from, independent of our interlocutor: a smile-in-itself, a terrifying smile, the mask that could cover any face: our own, for example.

GOGOL

Some authorities, though only some, make Gogol out to be a saint; others, more frequent, a ghost. "He seemed to me so little like a living being," Aksakov wrote the day after Gogol's death, "that though I am afraid of corpses and cannot bear to look at them, I experienced no such feeling beside his body."

Tormented by a chill that never left him, he was forever murmuring "my teeth are chattering, I'm freezing to death." He ran from country to country, consulted doctors, changed hospitals: no climate cured the chill inside. No liaison, no affair has ever been discovered. His biographers speak openly of his impotence. No flaw isolates more. Impotent, a man possesses the inner strength that makes him singular, inaccessible, and (paradoxically) dangerous: he frightens us. Animal quit of his animality, a man without a race, a life abandoned by instinct, he enriches himself by all he has lost: he is the mind's chosen victim. Can we conceive of an impotent rat? Rodents, indeed, perform the act in question capitally. We cannot say as much of men: the more exceptional they are, the more apparent this crucial failure that severs them from the chain of being. All activities are permitted them, save the one which links us to the zoological series. Sexuality is a great leveler; better, it strips us of our mystery . . . Much more than our other needs and endeavors, it is sexuality that puts us on an even footing with our kind: the more we practice it, the more we become like everyone else: it is in the performance of a reputedly bestial function that we prove our status as citizens: nothing is more *public* than the sexual act.

Abstinence—voluntary or forced—sets the individual both above and below the Species, makes him into an alloy of Saint and Imbecile that intrigues and abashes us. Whence our equivocal hatred for the Monk, as for any man who has renounced woman, who has renounced being *like us*. We shall never forgive him his solitude: it degrades as much as it disgusts us; it is a provocation. O the strange ascendancy of flaws! Gogol once confessed that love, had he yielded to it, would have "instantaneously reduced me to dust." Such an admission, as fascinating as it is dreadful, reminds us of Kierkegaard and his "thorn in the flesh." Yet the Danish philosopher's nature was an erotic one: his broken engagement, his debacle as a lover, tormented him all his life and tainted even his theological works. Can we then compare Gogol to Swift, that other "blasted" man? This would be to forget that the Dean, if he lacked the luck to love, possessed at least that of breaking hearts. To "place" Gogol, we must imagine a Swift with neither Stella nor Vanessa.

*

"The beings who live before our eyes in *The Inspector General* or in *Dead Souls*," one biographer observes, "are 'nothing.'" And being "nothing," they are "everything."

Indeed they lack "substance"; hence their universality. What are Chichikov, Pliushkin, Sobakeivitch, Nozdrev, Manilov, the heroes of *The Overcoat* or *The Nose*, if not ourselves reduced to our essence? "Null and void" Gogol calls his souls, yet they achieve a certain greatness: that of the banal. As if he were a Shakespeare of the shabby, a Shakespeare determined to observe our vagaries, our perverse obsessions, the warp of our days. No one has ventured further than Gogol into the perception of the commonplace. It is because of their reality that his characters become nonexistent, turn into symbols in which we recognize ourselves outright. They do not decline, for they had fallen from the start. We cannot help thinking of *The Possessed*; but where Dostoevsky's heroes fling themselves headlong toward their limits, Gogol's retreat to theirs; if the former seem to be answering an appeal that is beyond their powers, the latter heed only their incommensurable triviality.

In the last period of his life, Gogol was seized with remorse: his characters, he decided, were nothing but vice, vulgarity, filth. He would have to set about giving them virtues, wresting them from their ruin. So he wrote the Second Part of *Dead Souls*; fortunately, he threw it in the fire. His heroes could not be "saved." His gesture was imputed to madness, though it issued from the scruples of his artist's conscience: the writer triumphed over the prophet. It is Gogol's ferocity we prize, his contempt for men, the vision of a world condemned: how would we have endured an *edifying caricature?* An irreparable loss? Rather, a salutary one.

*

The Gogol of the last days is still visited by an obscure power he does not know how to use: he collapses into lethargy, shaken by spasms at long intervals: the spasms of a spectre. The humor that permitted him to keep his "anxiety attacks" at bay vanishes. A pitiful ordeal begins. His friends abandon him. He commits the folly of publishing the *Extracts from My Correspondence*, "a slap," as he admits, "at my public, my friends, and myself." Slavophiles and Occidentalists repudiate him. His book was an apology for power, for serfdom, a reactionary tract. To his misfortune, he befriends a certain Father Matvei, a narrow-minded, aggressive priest impervious to art, who gains a confessor's hold, a torturer's power over him. He carries this man's letters about with him, reading them over and over: a stupidity cure compared to which Pascal's *abêtissez-vous* looks like a whim. When a writer's gifts are exhausted, it is the ineptitudes of a spiritual director that come to fill the blanks of his inspiration. Father Matvei's influence over Gogol was more important than Pushkin's—the latter encouraged his genius, the priest set about smothering its last remains . . . Not content to preach, Gogol attempted to punish himself still further; his work had given the grimace a universal significance: his religious agonies were to feel its effects.

Some may claim that his miseries were deserved, that by them he expiated the insolence of having deformed the human face. The contrary seems more likely; he had to pay for seeing clearly. In art, it is not our errors for which we must atone but our "truths," what we have really witnessed. His characters pursued him. By his own admission, he carried the Klestakovs, the Chichikovs around with him forever: their subhumanity overwhelmed him. He had redeemed none of them; as an artist he could not. Now that he had lost his genius, he attempted to win his salvation. His heroes kept him from it. In spite of himself, he had to abide by their vacuity.

It is not the Regent Gogol suggests (who, Saint-Simon said, was "born bored"), not Baudelaire, not Ecclesiastes, not even the Devil's own unemployment had he lived in a world where evil did not exist; it is a being who turns his prayers against himself. At such a point, boredom acquires an almost mystical dignity. "Any absolute sensation," Novalis says, "is religious." In time, Gogol's boredom replaced his faith and became for him absolute sensation, religion.

VERBAL DEMIURGY

If I were asked what man I most envied, I should answer without hesitation: the one who, taking his ease among words, lives there naively, by reflex, neither questioning nor identifying them with signs, as if they corresponded to reality itself or as if they were an absolute strewn in the everyday. I should have, on the other hand, no reason for envying the man who sees through them, discerns their depths, their nothingness. For him, no spontaneous transactions with reality; isolated from his tools, pinioned to a dangerous autonomy, he attains to a selfhood which alarms him. Words flee him: unable to catch up, he pursues them with a nostalgic hatred and never proffers any without a sneer or a sigh. If he no longer communes with them, he still cannot do without them, and it is precisely at the moment when he is furthest from them that he clings to them most.

*

The discomfort which language provokes in us does not differ from the kind reality inspires; the void we glimpse at the bottom of words evokes the one we grasp in things: two perceptions, two experiences in which the disjunction operates between objects and symbols, between reality and signs. In the poetic act, this disjunction assumes the image of a rupture. Wresting himself by instinct from conventional meanings, from the inherited universe and the transmitted word, the poet, seeking another order, hurls a challenge to the nothingness of the evident, to the optical system as it is. He commits himself to a verbal demiurgy.

*

Let us imagine a world in which Truth, discovered at last, would be accepted by everyone, in which it would triumphantly whelm the charm of the proximate and the possible. Poetry would be inconceivable. But since, happily for poetry, our truths can scarcely be distinguished from fictions, poetry is not obliged to subscribe to them; it will therefore create a universe of its own, one as true, as false as our own. But not so extensive, nor so powerful. Number is on our side: we are legion, and our own conventions possess that force which only statistics confer. To these advantages we may add one more, and not the slightest: that of wielding a monopoly of worn-out words. The numerical superiority of our lies will always allow us to triumph over the poets, and will keep the debate open between the orthodoxy of discourse and the heresy of verse.

*

Once we yield to the temptation of skepticism, the exasperation produced by the employment of a utilitarian language diminishes and is converted in the long run into acceptance: we resign ourselves to it, we admit it. Since there is no more substance in things than in words, we accommodate ourselves to their improbability and—call it maturity or lassitude—renounce all intervention in the life of the Word: what is the use of lending it additional meaning, violating or renewing it, once we have discerned its nothingness? Skepticism: the smile that overhangs words

. . . After having weighed them one after the other, the operation over, we no longer think about them. As for "style," if we still sacrifice to it, only our idleness and imposture are responsible.

The poet judges differently: he takes language seriously, creates one for himself in his own way. All his singularities proceed from his intolerance of words as they are. Unfit to endure their banality and erosion, he is predestined to suffer from them and for them; yet it is by them that he tries to save himself, from their regeneration that he seeks his salvation. However grim his vision, he is never a true negator. To attempt to reinvigorate words, to infuse a new life into them supposes a fanaticism, an obnubilation beyond the line of duty: to invent—poetically—is to be an accomplice and a fanatic of the Word, a false nihilist: every verbal demiurgy is indulged at the expense of lucidity . . .

There is no use asking poetry to answer our questions or to afford some essential revelation. Its "mystery" is worth as much, and as little, as any other. Then why do we appeal to poetry? why—at certain moments—are we compelled to resort to it?

When, alone amid words, we are unable to communicate the slightest vibration to them, when they seem to us as dry, as degraded as ourselves, when the mind's silence is heavier than that of objects, we descend to the point where the dread of our inhumanity lays hold of us. Adrift, far from the evident, we suffer suddenly that horror of language which hurls us into silence—an instant of vertigo in which poetry alone can console us for the momentary loss of our certainties and our doubts. Hence it is the absolute of our *negative hours*—not of all our hours, but only of those which derive from our *malaise* in the verbal universe. Since the poet is a monster who risks his salvation by the word, and since he makes up for the universal void by the very symbol of the void (for is the word anything else?), why should we not follow him in his exceptional illusion? He becomes our recourse whenever we desert the fictions of ordinary language to seek other and unaccustomed, if not rigorous, ones. Does it not then seem that any other unreality is preferable to our own, and that there is more substance in a line of verse than in all those words trivialized by our conversations or our prayers? Whether poetry should be accessible or hermetic, effective or gratuitous, is a secondary problem. Exercise or revelation—what does it matter? All we ask of it is that it deliver us from the oppression, from the pangs of discourse. If it succeeds it supplies, *for a moment*, our salvation.

*

For contrary reasons, language is advantageous only to the vulgar and to the poet; if we profit by falling asleep over words or by fighting them, we run, on the other hand, some risk in sounding them out in order to discover their deception. The man who does so, who attends to them, who analyzes them, reaches the point of extenuating them, of transforming them into shadows. He will be punished for this, since he will share their fate. Take any word, repeat it a number of times, examine it: it will vanish, and in consequence something will vanish *in you*. Take more, and continue the operation. By degrees you will reach the culminating point of your sterility, the antipodes of a verbal demiurgy.

*

One does not withdraw one's confidence from words, nor violate their security, without setting one foot in the abyss. Their nothingness proceeds from our own. No longer united with our mind, it is as if they had never served us. Do they exist? We conceive their existence without feeling it. O the solitude in which they leave us, and in which we leave them! We are free, it is true, but we regret their despotism. They were here with things; now that they are disappearing, things are preparing to follow them and shrink before our eyes. Everything diminishes, everything is reabsorbed.

Where to escape, how flee the infinitesimal? Matter dwindles, abdicates its dimensions, vacates the premises . . . Yet our fear dilates and, occupying the terrain, serves as a universe.

IN SEARCH OF A NON-MAN

Cowards, we substitute for the sentiment of *our* nothingness the sentiment of nothingness. It is because the general void disquiets us not one whit: in it we see all too often a promise, a fragmentary absence, an impasse opening up . . .

For a long time I have searched for someone who would know everything about himself and about others, a demon-sage, divinely clairvoyant. Each time I believed I had found him, he obliged me, upon scrutiny, to sing a different tune: the new elect always possessed some flaw, some defect, some recess of unconsciousness or weakness which lowered him to the level of human beings. I perceived in him certain traces of desire and of hope, some hint of regret. His cynicism, manifestly, was incomplete. What a disappointment! And I still pursued my quest, and always my idols of the moment sinned in some direction: the *man* was always present in them, hidden, painted over or juggled out of sight. _ ended by understanding the despotism of the Race and no longer dreaming of a non-man, a monster who might be totally imbued with his nothingness. It was madness to conceive of him: he could not exist, absolutely lucidity being incompatible with the reality of the organs.

TO HATE ONESELF

Self-love is an easy thing: result of the instinct of self-preservation, the animals themselves would feel it if they were just a touch perverted. What is more difficult, and what man alone excels in, is self-hatred. Having expelled him from Paradise, it did its best to widen the gap separating him from the world, to keep him awake between moments, in the void which insinuates itself between them. It is from self-hatred that consciousness emerges, hence it is in self-hatred that we must seek the point of departure of the human phenomenon. I hate myself: I am absolutely a man. To be conscious is to be divided from oneself, is to hate oneself. This hatred seethes at our roots at the same time that it furnishes sap to the Tree of Knowledge.

Thus we have man outside the world, and remote from himself. We cannot (without abuse) classify him among the living, so superficial is his contact with life; his contact with death is no less so. Not having been able to find his exact place between the one and the other, he has cheated from the first: an intruder, a pseudo-animal, a false mortal, an impostor. Consciousness, that non-participation in what one is, that faculty of not coinciding with anything, was not provided for in the economy of creation. Man knows it, but he has neither the courage to assume it to the end and to die of it, nor to repudiate it in order to save himself. Alien to his nature, alone amid himself, detached from both the here at hand and the beyond, he espouses no reality utterly: how could he, when he is only half real? A being *without existence*.

Each step he takes in the direction of the mind is equivalent to a sin against life. In order to relate himself anew to *things*, why does he not put an end to the adventure of consciousness! But he is barred from that state of irreflection (in which his sentiment of guilt would cease) by a self-hatred from which he neither can nor will release himself. Stepping back from the line of other beings, leaving the beaten paths of salvation, he incessantly innovates in order to support his reputation as an *interesting* animal.

Consciousness, a provisional phenomenon if there ever was one, he manages to aggravate to its point of explosion, and to fall into fragments along with it. By destroying himself, he will raise himself to his essence, and he will fulfill his mission: to become his own enemy. If life has falsified matter, he has falsified life. Will his experiment be repeated? It does not seem to imply much of a posterity: everything leads us to assume that man is the last caprice nature has allowed herself.

MEANING OF THE MASK

However far our thought ventures, however detached it is from our interests, it still hesitates to call certain things by their names. Where our supreme terrors are concerned, the mind evades them, spares and flatters us. Thus, after so many ordeals, when "fate" reveals itself to us, our mind bids us see it as a limit, a reality beyond which any quest would be pointless. But is it really that limit, that reality, as our mind pretends? We doubt it, so suspect does our mind seem to us when it seeks to bind us here and impose a destiny upon us. We realize that there cannot be an end, and that through it is manifested another force, this one *supreme*. Whatever artifices and efforts our mind produces to dissimulate it, we end nonetheless by identifying it, by naming it even. Then what seemed to accumulate all the claims of reality is no longer anything but a face? A face? Not even that, but a disguise, a simple appearance used by this force to destroy us without *colliding with us*.

"Fate" was only a mask, as everything is a mask that is not death.

CONTAGION OF TRAGEDY

It is not pity, it is envy the tragic hero inspires in us, that lucky devil whose sufferings we devour as if we were entitled to them and he had cheated us of them. Why not try to take them back from him? In any case, they were meant for us . . . To be all the more certain of that, we declare them our own, aggrandize them and give them excessive proportions; grapple or groan before us as he will, he cannot move us, for we are not his spectators but his rivals, his competitors in the theatre, capable of supporting *his* miseries better than he is: taking them upon ourselves, we exaggerate them beyond his possibilities *on stage*. Armed with his fate and rushing toward his defeat faster than he, we spare him at most a superior smile, while we reserve to ourselves alone the merits of the fault or the murder, the remorse or the expiation. What is he beside us, and how ordinary his agony seems! Are we not laden with all his pains, do we not represent the victim he tried to incarnate without managing to do so? But, O mockery! at the end it is nonetheless *he* who dies!

OUTSIDE THE WORD

As long as we are enclosed within literature, we respect its truths and busy ourselves giving them body, padding their nothingness. A distressing condition, no doubt. But there is worse: to exceed those truths, without for all that embracing those of wisdom. What direction to take? what sector of the mind to settle for? One is no longer a *littérateur*; yet one writes, even while despising *expression*. To preserve the scraps of a vocation and lack the courage to rid oneself of it is an equivocal position, even a tragic one, which wisdom knows nothing about, for wisdom consists precisely in the audacity to extirpate every vocation, literary or otherwise. The man who has had the bad luck to be infected by Letters will retain forever the fetishism of the phrase, some superstition or other from which words alone will benefit. Possessing a talent he neglects or dreads, he will hurl himself without conviction into enterprises or works necessarily abortive, a spoiler suspended between speech and silence, a paltry creature pretending to that glory of the Void refused to whoever expresses himself or attaches himself to his own name. "Real life" is outside the word.

And yet the word obnubilates, dominates us: have we not gone so far as to make the universe itself rise out of it? Have we not identified our origins with the garrulity, the improvisations of a phrase-mongering god? To reduce cosmogony to discourse, to erect language into an instrument of the Creation, to attribute our origins to an illusory antiquity of the Word! Literature, we realize, reaches far back in time, since (never short of aberrations) we have not feared to impute to it the first convulsions of matter.

THE NECESSITY OF LYING

The man who has glimpsed, at the start of his career, certain mortal truths, reaches the point of no longer being able to live with them. If he remains loyal to them he is lost. To unlearn them, to renounce them—sole method of making up with life, of leaving the path of Knowledge, of the Intolerable. In pursuit of the lie, any lie which promotes action, he idolizes it and from it seeks his salvation. Any obsession seduces him, provided it smothers the demon of his curiosity and immobilizes his mind. Hence he envies all those who, by means of prayer or any other freak, have arrested the course of their thoughts, abdicated the responsibilities of the intellect and encountered, within a temple or a madhouse, the happiness of being *through*. What would he not give to be able to exult, like them, in the shadow of an error, in the shelter of a stupidity! He will try anything. "To elude my ruin, I shall play the game, I shall persevere out of stubbornness, out of whim, out of insolence. To breathe is an aberration which fascinates me. Air avoids me, the ground trembles under my feet. I have summoned every word and ordered them to dispose themselves into a prayer; and words have remained inert and mute. That is why I cry out, and continue to cry out: "Anything, except my truths!"

And now he is preparing to rid himself of them, to put them on the shelf. And while he celebrates a blindness so long desired, anxiety seizes upon him, courage abandons him: he fears the revenge of his knowledge, the return of his clairvoyance, the irruption of his certitudes, from which he had suffered so much. It is enough to make him lose all assurance: the road to salvation looks to him like a new Calvary.

FUTURE OF SKEPTICISM

Naiveté, optimism, generosity—we encounter them among botanists, specialists in the pure sciences, explorers, never among politicians, historians, or priests. Those in the first group do without their kind, those in the second make man the object of their activities or their investigations. We turn sour only in the vicinity of man. Those who devote their thoughts to him, examine him or try to help him, sooner or later come to despise him, hold him in horror. A psychologist if ever there was one, a priest is the most disabused human example, incapable by profession of putting the slightest trust in his fellow men; whence his knowing looks, his cunning, his phony kindness and his profound cynicism. Those priests—actually an infinitesimal group—who made their way to sanctity could not have reached it if they had observed their flocks more closely: they were strays, *bad* priests, unfit to live as voyeurs—and as parasites —of original sin.

To be cured of every illusion about man, one must possess the knowledge, the millennial experience of the confessional. The Church is so old and so disabused that it can no longer credit anyone's salvation, nor enjoy intolerance. After coming to grips with an incommensurable host of the fervent and the suspect, she was to end by fathoming them and wearying of them, by detesting their scruples, their torments, their avowals. Two thousand years among the secrecy of souls! It was too much, even for her. Miraculously preserved heretofore from the temptation of disgust, she yields to it now: the consciences whose charge she bears importune and overtax her. None of our miseries, none of our infamies any longer awaken her interest: we have worn out her pity and her curiosity. Since she knows so much about us all, she disdains us, lets us go, lets us look elsewhere . . . Already the fanatics are leaving her. Soon she will be the last refuge of skepticism.

VICISSITUDES OF FEAR

Since the Renaissance, science has undertaken to persuade us that we live in an indifferent nature, a world neither hostile nor favorable. A diminution of our stock of fear was to result. A considerable danger, for this fear was one of the *data*, one of the conditions of our existence and of our equilibrium.

Conferring intensity and vigor upon our moods, it sharpened our piety and our irony, our loves even as our hates, heightened and spiced each of our sensations. The more it spurred us on, the happier we were to be hunted creatures, greedy of uncertainties and dangers, of any occasion to triumph or to succumb. Without restraint, without ceremony, impertinent fear deployed its talents, its verve which we dreaded, which we cherished. Our enthusiasm for it increased in proportion to the *frissons* it afforded us. To escape its empire—who would have thought of such a thing? It governed us, subjugated us, while we delighted to see it presiding with such assurance over our victories and our defeats. Yet fear itself, which seemed preserved from all vicissitudes, was to suffer them, and indeed the cruelest of them all. Under the blows of a "progress" impatient to banish it, fear began, in the last century especially, to hide, to become timid and even sheepish, to withdraw, almost to vanish. Our century, more lucid than the last, finally grew alarmed: how, it asked, are we to rescue fear, restore its ancient status, recover its rights? Science itself took over: it became a threat, the source of terror. And we are now assured of possessing that quantity of fear indispensable to our prosperity.

A MAN WHO HAS ARRIVED

To the habitué, to the man intimate with the depths, "mystery" does not make much of an impression; he never speaks of it in any special way nor even knows what it is: he *lives* it . . . The reality in which he moves does not involve any other: no zone lower and beyond; he is lower than anything and beyond anything. Satiated on transcendence, superior to the operations of the mind and to the servitudes attached to them, he takes his ease on his inexhaustible lack of curiosity . . . Neither religion nor metaphysics intrigues him: what is there to fathom if he is already in the unfathomable? Fulfilled? Doubtless; but he does not know if he still exists.

We assert ourselves to the degree that, behind a given reality, we pursue another in which, beyond the absolute itself, we are still searching. Does theology stop with God? Not at all. It seeks to go further, just as metaphysics, poring over essences, never deigns to settle there. One like the other fears being anchored in a last principle, shifts from secret to secret, burns incense to the inexplicable and shamelessly abuses it. Mystery—what a windfall! But what a curse to suppose one has achieved it, to imagine one knows it and sojourns there! No longer a quest: it is here, within arm's reach. The arm of a dead man.

CRUMBS OF MELANCHOLY

1) Suddenly, falling short of everything, I creep toward the point of each object's *nonexistence*. The self: a label. Parallel to my face, I preen myself in my glances. Each thing is other, everything is other. Somewhere, an eye. Who

is watching me? I am frightened, and then I am outside my fear.

Outside moments and outside the subject I was, how am I to affiliate myself with time? Duration is mummified, becoming . . . has become. No longer a parcel of air to breathe or scream in. Breath is denied, ideas fall silent, the mind *was*. I have dragged every *yes* in the mud, and cling to the world no better than a ring on a skeleton's finger.

2) "Other people," a bum once told me, "get theirs from getting ahead; I get mine from falling behind." Lucky bum! I don't even fall behind; I remain . . . And reality itself remains, immobilized by my doubts. The more I feel about myself, the more I project into things and revenge myself on them for my uncertainties. Once everything stops, then I can neither conceive nor take one step farther toward any horizon at all. A prehistoric sloth nails me to *this* moment . . . And when, to shake it off, I waken my instincts, I fall into another sloth, into that tragic idleness which is called melancholy.

3) Horror of the flesh, of the organs, of each cell, primordial horror, chemical horror. Everything in me disintegrates, even this horror. In what grease, what pestilence the spirit has taken up its abode! This body, whose every pore eliminates enough stench to infect space, is no more than a mass of ordure through which circulates a scarcely less ignoble blood, no more than a tumor which disfigures the geometry of the globe. Supernatural disgust! No one approaches without revealing to me, despite himself, the stage of his putrefaction, the livid destiny which awaits him. Every sensation is sepulchral, every delight a dirge. What meditation, however somber, could rise to the conclusions—to the nightmare —of our pleasures? The true metaphysicians are found among the debauchees, not elsewhere. It is by extenuating, by martyrizing our senses that we realize our nothingness, the abyss our frolics conceal for a moment. Too pure and too recent,

the mind cannot save this old flesh, whose corruption prospers before our eyes. Contemplating it, our cynicism itself retreats and collapses into tears. We deserve other torments, a spectacle less intolerable. In truth, there is no salvation by our bodies, nor by our souls either. If I were to draw up the inventory of my days, I should doubtless find none which failed to supply, by itself, the requirements of several hells.

It is said in the Apocalypse that the worst torments await those whose foreheads are not marked by the "seal of God." All will be spared, except these. Their sufferings will resemble those of a man stung by scorpions, and they will seek death in vain, the death which is nonetheless within them . . .

Not to be marked by the "seal of God." How well I understand that, how well I understand that!

4) I think of that emperor dear to my heart, Tiberius, of his acrimony and his ferocity, his obsession with islands, his boyhood in Rhodes, his old age on Capri. I love him because his *neighbor* seemed to him inconceivable, I love him because he loved no one. Fleshless, pimply, an icy monster whom terror alone could warm, he had a passion for exile: as if he figured at the head of his own list of proscriptions . . . To feel he was alive, he had to know terror and to inspire it: if he feared everyone, he demanded in his turn that everyone fear him. That seesawing between Capri and the suburbs of a Rome he dared not enter, that aversion faces inspired in him . . . As lonely as Swift, that pamphleteer of another age, that pamphleteer anterior to man. When everything leaves me, when I *leave myself*, I think of them both, I cling to their disgusts and to their cruelty, support myself on their vertigo. When I leave myself, yes, I turn to them: nothing then could separate me from their solitude.

5) For some, happiness is a sensation so unaccustomed that once they experience it they grow frightened and interrogate themselves about their new condition; nothing of the

kind is to be found in their past: it is the first time they have emerged from the security of *the worst*. An unexpected light makes them tremble, as if suns hung from their fingers to illuminate one crumbled paradise after another. This happiness from which they hoped for their deliverance—why does it assume such a countenance? What to do? Perhaps it does not belong to them, perhaps it has fallen to them by mistake. Stunned and fascinated both, they try to incorporate it into their nature, to possess it, if possible, forever. They are so ill-prepared for it that, to enjoy it, they must annex it to their old terrors.

6) Faith itself solves nothing: you bring to it your inclinations and your defects; if you are happy, it will increase the quantity of happiness you received as your birthright; if you are by nature unhappy, it will represent for you only an additional laceration, only a deterioration of your state: an *infernal* faith. Forever excluded from paradise, you will suffer a nostalgia for it like a further torment—one torture more. You pray: your prayers, instead of lightening them, will aggravate both your remorse and your sufferings. In truth, each of us rediscovers in his faith what he put into it: by faith the elect savors his salvation the more, the damned sinks only deeper into his hell. Who would ever suppose it suffices to believe in order to triumph over the insoluble? There is no faith, there are only multiple and irreconcilable forms of faith. Expect no help from yours, whatever it is: it will permit you only to be a little more what you have always been . . .

7) Our pleasures are not lost, nor do they disappear; in another way, they mark us as much as our pains. The one among them which seemed to have vanished forever will save us from a crisis, will plead, unknown to us, against one of our disappointments, against some temptation to abdicate, to surrender; it will create in us new links of which we are not conscious, and reinforce a heap of little hopes which will counterbalance that tendency of our memory to pre-

serve only vestiges of the atrocious, the terrible. For our memory is a venal thing: it sides with our pains, it has *sold itself* to our sufferings.

8) According to Cassian, Evagrus, and Nilus of Ancyra, no demon is more redoubtable than the demon of *acedia.* The monk who succumbs to it will be its victim to the end of his days. Glued to the window, he will stare outside, will await visits, any visits, in order to palaver, to forget himself.

To strip oneself of everything and then discover one had taken the wrong path, to cool one's heels in solitude and be unable to leave it! For every hermit who has succeeded, there are a thousand who have failed. These defeated men, these failures steeped in the ineffectiveness of their prayers —the Church sought to revive them by song, imposed upon them exultation, the discipline of joy. Victims of the demon, how could they have raised their voices, and to whom? As remote from Grace as from the age, they spent hours comparing their sterility to that of the desert, to the material image of their void.

Glued to my window, to what would I compare my sterility if not to that of the City? Yet the *other* desert, the real one, haunts me. If only I could go there and forget the odor of men! As God's neighbor, I should inhale His desolation and His eternity that I dream of at the moments there awakens in me the memory of a distant cell. In a previous life, what monastery did I abandon or betray? My incompleted prayers, broken off then, pursue me now, while in my brain some heaven or other appears and disappears.

9) Ali! Ali! A dervish, having renounced dealings with all words except that one, never utters another, in any circumstance. This was the sole infraction he allowed himself of his regime of silence.

Prayer: a concession made to God, certain *phrases,* and all the complacency which they presume. Our dervish, immolating himself in the essential, sacrificed language, that symbol of appearance; every man who resorts to it turns away from the absolute, even if he mortifies himself else-where or subscribes to the enormities of faith. Every man and *a fortiori*, every saint. Francis of Assisi was a chatter-box like his disciples, like his rivals. Only one thing matters, only one word. If we speak, it is because we have not found that thing, nor shall find it.

10) Only the man who strives to fail deserves our trust: if he succeeds in this he will have killed the monster, *the monster he was* as long as he was concerned to act, to triumph. We progress only to the detriment of our purity, that *summa* of our setbacks. Sustained, traversed by an impulse toward corruption, our actions preclude us from paradise, fortify our failure, our fidelity to the world: no movement forward which does not excite and consolidate in us the old perversion of existence.

To take leave of beings is not enough; one must also take leave of things, execrate and abolish them one by one. To recover our first absence, let us follow our cosmogonies in reverse and, since the modesty of dying fails us, let us an-nihilate at least every trace in ourselves of the here and now, down to the last memory of what we were. May some god grant us the power to resign from everything, to betray everything, the audacity of an unspeakable cowardice!

ORGY OF VACUITY

Powerless to leave the sphere of his inclinations, the artist moves in a narrow sector of existence. He wears blinkers: his talent is his infirmity. Even when he has genius, he still remains captive of his optics, of the misfortune which has provided him with a *finite* vision.

What an advantage to be gifted for nothing, what a free-dom! Everything is offered to you, everything belongs to you; dominating space, you pass from one object to the next, from one world to the next. The universe at your feet, you accede at once to the essence of happiness: exaltation at the zero point of Being, life transposed, promoted to the state of breath, of eternity, which breathes and which no mystery burdens.

Obliged to be everywhere, a slave of His ubiquity, God Himself is a prisoner. Freer, more untrammeled than He, you delight in absence, whose extent you explore at your pleasure: impoverished substance, inaudible sigh, delight in losing the *praxis* of both life and death.

*

Every talented man deserves commiseration: what will the painter derive, once more, from his colors? How will the poet awaken his exhausted words? And what can we say of the musician's prospects in a world where every combination of sounds has been imagined? Profoundly unfortunate, all are engaged in the inextricable. We must lavish upon them an extra ration of solicitude, not insult their confusion, so that they may forget the impasse of their art, their condition of disinheritance.

Without going so far as to trumpet our fortune, we cannot, however, pass it over in silence. Let us thank Providence for having released us from the burden, the fatalities of a talent. By stripping us of everything, it has thereby offered us everything. Whether our fulfilled destitution emanates from Its pity or Its negligence, our lights do not permit us to decide. Still, the fact is that Providence has granted us an unparalleled favor: are we not pledged all the talents we lack? To be nothing—infinite resource, perpetual feast.

*

Never at rest, the artist must sustain his disorders, waste his strength, create his own happiness and misery, *produce*. Whereas the sage, since he engages in no work, occupies himself with sterility, accumulates energy he never expends. Truth he acquires to the detriment of the *expressed*, of communication, of all which nourishes and justifies art, that obstacle to the true, that vehicle of lies. Smothering his faculties of invention, he governs his actions and his movements, repulses the services of trance and of fever. (There is no *inspired* sage.) Neither tragedy, which is the lust for laceration, nor history, which is the focus of that lust, engages his curiosity: having transcended both, he rejoins the elements, refuses to create, to copy God or the Devil, and devotes himself to a long meditation on the angel and the idiot, on the excellence of their hebetude, which he would attain by *the means of lucidity*.

It is the characteristic of the "creator," after having abused his resources, to exhaust himself: his powers abandon him, the intensity of his obesssions diminishes. If he preserves his vitality or his reason, the same is not true of his capacity to vibrate, his sympathy. His old age is truly endless. The sage, on the contrary, triumphs at the end of his days, fulfills himself *in extremis*. We cannot imagine him *finished*; this adjective applies, from a certain moment, to every artist. An *oeuvre* answers to an appetite for self-destruction and is constructed to the detriment of a life. The sage does not know such an appetite, or has conquered it. His greatest ambition: to disappear without leaving a trace. But there is such power in his will to effacement that he intrigues us. We find it very difficult to penetrate his secret: how to exist without destroying oneself at every moment? And yet this secret can be glimpsed when we approach ourselves, our ultimate reality. Words, then, losing all utility, all meaning, appear to us as the agents of an immemorial vulgarity. Everything changes, down to our way of seeing, as if our glances, piled upon themselves, possessed a universe distinct from that of matter. In point of fact, this world no longer enters the field of our perceptions, nor is perpetuated by our memory. Turned toward what does not support the word nor seek to condescend to it, we loll in a happiness without qualities, in a *frisson* without adjectives. A siesta in God . . .

THE TEMPTATION TO EXIST

SOME men make their way from affirmation to affirmation, their life a series of acceptances . . . Forever applauding reality or what passes for it in their eyes, they accept the universe and are not ashamed to say so. There is no contradiction they cannot resolve or relegate to the category of "the way things turn out." The more they let themselves be contaminated by philosophy, the more they pride themselves, faced with the entertainments of life and death, on being a *good audience*.

For others, habitual nay-sayers, affirmation demands not only deliberate self-deception but self-sacrifice as well: how much effort the merest nod to existence can cost! What repudiations must be renounced! They know there is never just one "yes": each assent implies another, perhaps a whole parade—who can afford to take such risks lightly? Yet the security of negation aggravates the nay-sayers, too, and hence they conceive the necessity and the interest of affirming something—anything.

It is true that negation is the mind's first freedom, yet a negative habit is fruitful only so long as we exert ourselves to overcome it, adapt it to our needs; once *acquired* it can imprison us—a chain like any other. And slavery for slavery, the servitude of existence is the preferable choice, even at the price of a certain self-splintering: it is a matter of avoiding the contagion of nothingness, the comforts of the abyss . . .

*

For centuries theologians have told us that hope is the daughter of patience. And of modesty as well, one might add; the man of pride has no *time* for hope . . . Unwilling and unable to wait for their culmination, he violates events as much as he violates his own nature; bitter, tainted, when he exhausts his rebellion he abdicates his existence—for him there is no intermediate formula. His lucidity is undeniable, but let us remember that lucidity is a condition peculiar to those who by their incapacity to love are as isolated from others as from themselves.

The assent to death is the greatest one of all. It can be expressed in several ways . . .

There are among us daylight ghosts, devoured by their absence, for whom life is one long aside. They walk our streets with muffled steps, and look at no one. No anxiety can be discovered in their eyes, no haste in their gestures. For them an outside world has ceased to exist, and they submit to every solitude. Careful to keep their distance, solicitous of their detachment, they inhabit an undeclared universe situated somewhere between the memory of the unimaginable and the imminence of certainty. Their smile suggests a thousand vanquished fears, the grace that triumphs over all things terrible: such beings can pass through matter itself. Have they overtaken their own origins? Discovered in themselves the very sources of light? No defeat, no victory disturbs them. Independent of the sun, they are self-sufficient: illuminated by Death.

*

We are not in a position to identify the moment when the operations of erosion occur within us at the expense of our human substance. We know only that the result of such operations is a void, into which the idea of our own destruction gradually settles. A vague, faintly outlined idea: as if the void were aware of itself. Then from the furthest reaches of the self, in sonorous transfiguration, may be heard a noise, a sound, a *tonality* which by its very insistence must either paralyze us forever or preserve our life anew. We may find ourselves captives of fear or of nostalgia; lower than death or on its own level. Captives of fear, if this tonality merely perpetuates the void in which it occurs; and of nostalgia, if it converts the void to plenitude. According to our structure, we shall discern in death either a deficit or a surplus of being.

*

Before affecting our perception of duration—acquired relatively late—the fear of death attacks our sense of dimension, of immediacy—our illusion of what is *solid*: space shrinks, shoots from our grasp, turns into thin air, becomes entirely transparent. Our fear replaces space, welling up until it obscures the very reality that provoked it—until it substitutes itself for death. All experience is suddenly reduced to an exchange between the self and this fear, which, as an autonomous reality, isolates us in such unmotivated terrors, such gratuitous shudders that we run the risk of forgetting we are going to . . . die. Yet fear can supplant our real problems only to the extent that we—unwilling either to assimilate or to exhaust it—perpetuate it within ourselves like a temptation and enthrone it at the very heart of our solitude. One step further and we shall become debauchees not of death but of the fear of death. Such is the history of all the fears we have not been able to overcome: no longer subservient to motivation, they grow into independent, tyrannical idols. "We live in fear, and therefore we do not live." Buddha's words may be taken to mean that instead of keeping ourselves at the stage of being where fear opens out onto the world, we make it an end in itself, a closed universe, a substitute for *space*. If fear controls us, it must distort our image of the world. The man who can neither master nor exploit his fear ultimately ceases to be himself, loses his identity, for fear is valuable only if one defends oneself against it; the man who surrenders to it can never recover, but must proceed, in all transactions with himself, from treason to treason until he smothers death itself beneath his fear of it.

*

The attraction of certain problems derives from their lack of rigor, and hence from the contradictory solutions they provoke: so many more difficulties to entice the amateur of the Insoluble.

In order to "document" myself on the subject of death, a biological treatise is of no more use than the catechism: as far as *I* am concerned, it is a matter of indifference whether I am going to die because of original sin or the dehydration of my cells. Entirely independent of our intellectual system, death, like every individual experience, can be confronted only by knowledge without *information*. Hence many uneducated men have spoken more pertinently of it than this or that metaphysician; once experience has detected the agent of their destruction, such men devote all their thoughts to it, so that death becomes no mere impersonal "problem" but a reality all their own, *their death*.

Yet among all those who, uneducated or not, think continually of death, most do so only because they are terrified by the prospect of their final agony, not realizing that even if they were to live centuries, millennia, the *reasons* for their fear would remain entirely unchanged, agony being merely an accident in the process of our annihilation, a process that is, after all, co-extensive with our duration. Life, far from being what Bichat once called an ensemble of functions for resisting death, is rather an ensemble of functions for bearing us toward it. Our substance diminishes with every step, yet it is of this very diminution that all our efforts should tend to make a stimulant, a principle of efficacity. Those who cannot benefit from their possibilities of nonexistence are strangers to themselves: puppets, objects "furnished" with a self, numbed by a neutral time that is neither duration nor eternity. To exist is to profit by our share of unreality, to be quickened by each contact with the void that is within. To this void the puppet remains insensible, abandons it, permits it to decay, to die out . . .

*

A kind of germinative regression, a return to our roots, death destroys our identity only to permit us a surer access to it—a reconstitution; for death has no meaning unless we accord it all the attributes of life.

Although at our first, our primary perceptions of its quality, death presents itself as a dislocation, a loss, it subsequently produces, by revealing the nullity of time and the infinite worth of each separate moment, certain tonic effects: if it offers us only the image of our own inanity, by the same token it converts that inanity into an absolute, inviting us to commit ourselves to it. And by thus rehabilitating our "mortal" aspect, death institutes itself as a day-by-day dimension of our life, a triumphal agony.

What is the good of fastening our thoughts upon some tomb or other, staking anything upon our eventual rot? Spiritually degrading, the macabre confronts us with the exhaustion of our glands, the stinking garbage of our dissolution. We can claim to be alive only to the degree that we slight or circumvent the idea of our eventual corpse. Nothing of value results from reflections on the material fact of dying. If I permitted the flesh to dictate its philosophy, to impose its conclusions upon me, I might as well do away with myself before knowing them. For everything the flesh has to teach me annihilates me without recourse: does it not refuse all illusion? Does it not, as the interpreter of our ashes, continually contradict our lies, our fantasies, our hopes? Let us therefore proceed beyond its arguments, and force it to join battle against its own evidence.

To rejuvenate ourselves at the contact of death is a matter of investing it with all our energies, of becoming, like Keats, "half in love with easeful death" or, like Novalis, of making of death the principle that "romanticizes" life. If Novalis was to carry his nostalgia for death to the point of sensuality, it was Kleist who was to derive from it a completely inner "felicity." "*Ein Strudel von nie geahnter Seligkeit hat mich ergriffen . . .*" (A whirlpool of undreamed-of felicity has seized me), he writes, before committing suicide. Neither defeat nor abdication, his death was a rage of happiness, an exemplary and concerted madness, one of the rare successes of despair. Schlegel's remark that Novalis was the first man to experience death "as an artist" seems to me to apply more exactly to Kleist, who was better equipped for death than anyone has ever been. Unequaled, perfect, a masterpiece of tact and taste, his suicide makes all others unnecessary.

*

A vernal annihilation, culmination rather than chasm, death dizzies us only to raise us all the more readily above our customary selves, with the same privilege as love's, to which it is related in more than one respect: both love and death, applying an explosive pressure upon the framework of our lives, disintegrate us, fortify us, ruin us by the distractions of plenitude. As irreducible as they are inseparable, their elements constitute a fundamental equivocation. If, to a certain point, love destroys us, with what sensations of expansion and pride it does its work! And if death destroys us altogether, what *frissons* does it not employ! Sensations, shudders by which we transcend the *man* within us, and the accidents of the self.

Since both love and death define us only to the degree that we project our appetites and impulses upon them, that we cooperate wholeheartedly with their equivocal nature, they are necessarily beyond our grasp as long as we regard them as exterior realities, accessible to the operations of the intellect. We plunge into love as into death, we do not reflect upon them. For that matter, every experience that is not converted into a voluptuous one is a failure. If we had to limit ourselves to our sensations as they were, they would appear intolerable for being too distinct, too dissimilar from our essence. Death would not be the Great Human Experiment that Failed if men knew how to assimilate it to their nature or how to transform it into pleasure. But death remains within them as an experience *apart*, different from what they are.

And it is still another indication of the double reality of death—its equivocal character, the paradox inherent in the manner we experience it—that it presents itself to us as a *limit* and at the same time as a *datum*. We rush toward it, and yet we are already there. Thus even as we are incorporating it within our lives, we cannot keep ourselves from positing it in the future. By an inevitable inconsistency, we interpret death as the future which destroys the present, our present. If fear assisted us in defining our sense of space, it is death which reveals the true meaning of our temporal dimension, since without death, being in time would mean nothing to us, or, at the most, the same thing as being in eternity. Hence the traditional image of death, despite all our efforts to elude it, obstinately haunts us, an image for which sick men are chiefly responsible. In such matters we agree to recognize their qualifications; a prejudice in their favor automatically accords them a kind of "profundity," although most of them give every evidence of a disconcerting futility. We have all known *operetta incurables*.

More than anyone else the sick man is expected to identify himself with death; yet he does his utmost to detach himself from it, to project death outside himself. Since it is easier for him to run away from it than to confess its presence in himself, he uses every artifice to rid himself of death. He makes a practice, even a doctrine out of his defensive reaction. The ordinary man, in good health, is delighted to imitate him in every detail. And only the ordinary man? The mystics themselves employ subterfuges, practice every form of evasion, flight tactics: for them death is only an obstacle to be surmounted, a barrier which separates them from God, a last step in duration. In this life, they sometimes manage—thanks to ecstasy, that springboard— to leap beyond time: an instantaneous trajectory by which they achieve only "fits" of beatitude. They must disappear for good if they would attain the object of their desires; hence they love death because it permits them to realize these desires, and they hate death because it delays so long in coming. The soul, according to Theresa of Avila, aspires only to its creator, but "it sees at the same time that it is impossible to possess its creator if it does not die; and since it is impossible for the soul to put itself to death, it dies of the desire to die, until it is actually in danger of death." Always this need to make death into an accident or a means, to reduce it to a disappearance instead of regarding it as a presence—always this need to dispossess death. And if religions have made of it only a pretext or a scarecrow—a weapon of propaganda—it is the duty of the unbelievers to see that justice is done, to re-establish death and to restore all its rights.

Each being *is* his sentiment of death: It follows that the experiences of sick men and mystics cannot be discarded as false, although we may question their interpretations of these experiences. We are on ground where no criterion functions, where certitudes swarm, where everything is a certitude, because our truths here coincide with our sensations, our problems with our attitudes. Furthermore, what "truth" can we claim, when at every moment we are engaged in another experience of death? Our "destiny" itself is only the development, the phases of this primordial and yet changing experience, the translation into apparent time of that *secret time* in which the diversity of our ways of dying is elaborated. To explain a destiny, biographers should abandon their usual procedure, should give up examining this apparent time, this readiness of their subject to deteriorate his own essence. The same thing is true for a whole epoch: to know its institutions and its dates is less important than to divine its intimate experience of which these are the signs. Battles, ideologies, heroism, sanctity, barbarism —all so many simulacra of an interior world which alone should solicit our attention. Every culture dies out in its own way, every culture perfects several rules of extinction and imposes them upon its members: even the best among them could not change or evade such rules. A Pascal, a Baudelaire circumscribe death: one reduces it to our search for salvation, the other to our physiological terrors. If death overwhelms man, crushes him, it remains no less, for them both, *within* man. Quite the contrary, the Elizabethans or the German Romantics made of death a cosmic phenomenon, an orgiastic metamorphosis, a vivifying nothingness—ultimately a *force* in which man was to steep himself and with which it was important to maintain direct relations. For the Frenchman, what counts is not death in itself—an evidence of Matter's absentmindedness or merely an impropriety—but our behavior in the eyes of our fellow-men, the strategy of *adieux*, the countenance which the calculations of our vanity impose upon us—in short, *attitude*; not our quarrel with ourselves, but with others: a spectacle in which it is essential to observe the details and the motives. The whole of French art consists of knowing how to die *in public*. Saint-Simon describes not the agony of Louis XIV, of Monsieur, or of the Regent, but the *scenes* of their agony. The customs of the Court, an awareness of its ceremony, its ostentation, have been inherited by a whole people enamored of display and anxious to associate a certain brilliance with the last breath. In this regard Catholicism has been useful to the French: does it not maintain that the way we die is essential to our salvation, that our sins can be redeemed by a "good death"? A questionable notion, but one entirely adapted to a nation's histrionic instinct, and which, in the past more than today, is related to conceptions of honor and dignity, to the style of the *honnête homme*. It was then a question, setting God aside, of saving face in front of an audience, in front of the elegant strollers and gapers and the worldly confessors; not of perishing, but of *officiating*, preserving one's reputation before witnesses and asking extreme unction of them alone . . . Even the worst libertines died decorously, so much did their respect for opinion prevail over the irreparable, so much did they conform to the usages of an epoch in which to die signified, for man, to renounce solitude and privacy alike, to go on parade one last time, and in which the French were the greatest of all specialists in agony.

*

It is nevertheless doubtful that by relying on the "historical" aspect of the experience of death we shall manage to penetrate further into its original character, for history is merely an inessential mode of being, the most effective form of our infidelity to ourselves, a metaphysical refusal, a mass of events with which we confront the only event that matters. Everything that aims at affecting man—religions included—is tainted with a crude sentiment of death. And it is to seek a true, purer sentiment of this kind that the hermits took refuge in the desert, that negation of history which they rightly compared to the angels, since—they maintained—both were unaware of sin and the Fall into the realm of time. The desert, in fact, provides the image of duration translated into coexistence: a motionless flow, a metamorphosis bewitched by space. The solitary retires there less to expand his solitude and enrich his absence than to produce within himself the tonality of death.

In order to hear this tonality we must institute a desert within ourselves . . . If we succeed, certain harmonies flow through our blood, our veins dilate, our secrets and our resources appear upon the surface of ourselves where desire and disgust, horror and rapture mingle in obscure and luminous festivity. The dawn of death breaks within us: cosmic trance, the bursting of the spheres, a thousand voices! We are death, and everything is death—death seduces us, sweeps us away, carries us aloft, casts us to earth, or hurls us beyond the bounds of space itself. Death, forever intact, unworn by all the ages of our history, makes us accomplices in its apotheosis: we feel its immemorial freshness, and its time unlike any other . . . death's time, which ceaselessly creates and decomposes us. To such a degree does death hold us, immortalize us in agony, that we shall never be able to indulge ourselves in the luxury of dying; and although we possess the very science of destiny, although we are a veritable encyclopedia of fatalities, we nevertheless know nothing, for it is death that knows everything within us.

*

I often remember how, at the end of my adolescence, enmeshed in mortuary considerations, enslaved by a single obsession, I apprenticed myself to every force that invalidated my existence. My other thoughts no longer interested me: I knew too well *where* they led me, upon what they converged. From the moment I had only one problem, what was the use of concerning myself with *problems?* Ceasing to live in terms of a self, I gave death enough rope for my own enslavement; in other words, I no longer belonged to myself. My terrors, even my name were borne by death, and by substituting itself for my own eyes, death revealed to me in all things the marks of its sovereignty. In each man I passed I discerned a cadaver, in each odor a rot, in each joy a last grimace. Everywhere I stumbled against future victims of the noose, against their imminent shadows: other men's lives wore no mystery for The One who scrutinized them through my eyes. Was I bewitched? I preferred to think so. From now on what was I to do? The Void was my eucharist: everything within me, everything exterior to me was transubstantiated into a ghost. Irresponsible, at the antipodes of consciousness, I ended up by delivering myself to the anonymity of the elements, to the drunkenness of indivisibility, determined not to reintegrate my being nor to become again a colonist of chaos.

Unable to see in death the positive expression of the void, the agent that awakens the creature from itself, the summons resounding in the ubiquity of drowsiness, I knew nothingness by heart, and I accepted my knowledge. Even now, how could I mistake the auto-suggestion that produced the universe? Yet I protest against my own lucidity. I must have Reality at any price. I have feelings only out of cowardice; very well, I wish to be a coward, to impose a "soul" upon myself, to let myself be devoured by a thirst for immediacy, to destroy all my evidence and find myself a world whatever the cost. And if I could not find a world, I would content myself with a shard of being, with the illusion that something exists, whether before my eyes or somewhere else. I would be the conquistador of a continent of lies. To be duped or die: there was no other choice. Like those who have discovered life by the detours of death, I would hurl myself upon the first deception, upon anything that might restore my lost reality.

*

After the banality of the abyss, what miracles in being! Existence is the unheard of, *what cannot happen*, a state of exception. And nothing can engage it save our desire to accede to it, to force an entrance, to take it by assault.

To exist is a habit I do not despair of acquiring. I shall imitate the others, the cunning ones who have managed it, the turncoats of lucidity; I shall rifle their secrets, even their hopes, quite happy to snatch with them at the indignities that lead to life. Denial is beyond my strength, or my patience; assent tempts me. Having exhausted my reserves of negation, and perhaps negation itself, why should I not run out into the street shouting at the top of my lungs that I am on the verge of discovering a truth, the only one that is worth anything? But I do not know yet what that truth is; I know only the joy which precedes it, the joy and the madness and the fear.

It is this ignorance—and not fear of ridicule—that robs me of the courage to rouse the world with my news, to observe the world's terror at the spectacle of my happiness, of my definitive assent, my fatal *yes*.

*

Since we derive our vitality from our store of madness, we have only the certitudes and therapeutics of delirium with which to oppose our dread and our doubt. By dint of unreason, let us become a source, an origin, a starting point —let us multiply by all possible means our *cosmogonic moments*. We actually exist only when we radiate time itself, when suns rise within us and we dispense their light, illuminating the hours . . . It is then that we share in the volubility of things which are so astonished to have come into being and so impatient to broadcast their surprise in the metaphors of light. Everything swells and dilates to acquire the habit of the unexpected. A generation of miracles: everything converges upon us, for everything radiates from us. But can this really be us—ourselves? Of our own will? Can the mind conceive so much of day, time suddenly made eternal? And what brings to birth within us this quivering space, these roaring equators?

To think we could free ourselves of our penchant for agony, of our oldest evidence, would be to deceive ourselves about our capacity for aberration. In fact, after the favor of a few bits of being, we relapse into panic and disgust, into the temptations of melancholia and the cadaver, into the deficit of being that results from the negative sentiment of death. However serious our fall, it may nevertheless be useful to us if we turn it into a discipline that can induce us to reconquer the privileges of delirium. The hermits of the first centuries of Christianity will serve us again as an example. They will teach us how, in order to raise our psychic level, we must join a permanent combat with ourselves. It is with singular appropriateness that one Father of the Church has called them "athletes of the desert." They were warriors whose state of tension, whose relentless struggles against themselves we can scarcely imagine. There were some who recited up to seven hundred prayers a day; they kept track by dropping a pebble after each one . . . A mad arithmetic which made me admire them all the more for their matchless pride. They were not weaklings, these obsessed saints at grips with the dearest of all their possessions: *their temptations.* Living only in their behalf, they exacerbated these temptations to have still more to struggle against. Their descriptions of "desire" display such violence of tone that they scrape our senses raw and give us shudders no libertine author succeeds in inspiring. They were ingenious at glorifying "the flesh" in reverse. If it fascinated them to such a degree, what merit in having fought against its attractions! They were titans, more frenzied, more perverse than those of mythology; for the latter would never have been able, in their simplicity of mind, to conceive, for the accumulation of energy, all the advantages of self-loathing.

*

Our unprovoked natural sufferings being far too incomplete, it is up to us to augment, to intensify them, to create others for ourselves—artificial ones. Left to itself, the flesh encloses us within a narrow horizon. Only if we put it to the torture will it sharpen our perceptions and enlarge our perspectives: the mind is the result of the torments the flesh undergoes or inflicts upon itself. The anchorites knew how to remedy the insufficiency of their ills . . . After having joined battle with the world, they had to declare war against themselves. What tranquility for their neighbors! Does our ferocity not derive from the fact that our instincts are all too interested in other people? If we attended more to ourselves and became the center, the object of our own murderous inclinations, the sum of our intolerances would diminish. We shall never be able to estimate the number of horrors which those primitive monkish colonies spared humanity. Had all those hermits remained in the secular world, how many excesses would they not have committed! For the greatest good of their time, they had the inspiration to exercise their cruelty upon themselves. If we would moderate our manners, we must learn to turn our talons inward, to develop the technique of the desert . . .

*

Why, you ask, exalt this leprosy, these repulsive exceptions with which ascetic literature has gratified us? We must cling to whatever we have. At the same time that I execrate the monks and their convictions, I cannot help but admire their extravagances, their willful character, their asperity. There must be a secret in so much energy: the secret of religions themselves. And although they are perhaps not worth troubling about, the fact remains that everything that lives, every rudiment of existence, participates in a religious essence. Let us speak plainly: everything which keeps us from self-dissolution, every lie which protects us against our unbreatheable certitudes is religious. When I grant myself a share in eternity, when I conceive of a permanence which includes me, I trample underfoot the evidence of my friable, worthless being, I lie to the others as to myself. Were I to do otherwise, I should disappear within an hour. We last only as long as our fictions. When we see through them, our capital of lies, our religious holdings collapse. To exist is equivalent to an act of faith, a protest against the truth, an interminable prayer . . . As soon as they consent to live, the unbeliever and the man of faith are fundamentally the same, since both have made the only decision that defines a *being*. Ideas, doctrines—mere façades, decorative fantasies, accidents. If you have not resolved to kill yourself, there is no difference between you and the others, you belong to the faction of the living, all—no matter what their convictions —great believers. Do you deign to breathe? You are approaching sainthood, you deserve canonization . . .

Moreover, if you are dissatisfied with yourself, if you want to change your nature, you engage yourself twice over in an act of faith: you desire two lives within one. Which is precisely what our ascetics are attempting when, by making of death a means of not dying, they take pleasure in their vigils, their cries, their nocturnal athleticism. By imitating their excesses, even outstripping them, the day will come, perhaps, when we shall have mistreated our reason as much as they did. "I am guided by whoever is madder than myself"—thus speaks our thirst. Only our flaws, the opacities of our clairvoyance, can save us: were that transparence perfect, it would strip us of the senseless creature which inhabits us, the self to whom we owe the best of our illusions and our conflicts.

Since every form of life betrays and corrupts Life, the man who is genuinely alive assumes a maximum of incompatibilities, works relentlessly at pleasure and pain alike, espousing the nuances of the one as of the other, refusing all *distinct* sensations and every unmingled state. Our inmost aridity results from our allegiance to the rule of the *definite*, from our plea in bar of imprecision, that innate chaos which by renewing our deliriums keeps us from sterility. And it is against this beneficent factor, against this chaos, that every school of thought, every philosophy reacts. And if we do not succor it with all our solicitude, we shall waste our last reserves: those which sustain and stimulate our death within us, preventing it from growing old.

*

After having made of death an affirmation of life, having converted its abyss into a salutary fiction, having exhausted our arguments against the evidence, we are ambushed by stagnation, depression: it is the revenge of our accumulated bile, of our nature, of this demon of common sense which, allayed for a time, awakens to denounce the ineptitude and the absurdity of our will to blindness. A whole past of merciless vision, of complicity with our ruin, of accustoming ourselves to the venom of truth, and so many years of contemplating our remains in order to extract from them the principle of our knowledge! Yet we must learn to think against our doubts and against our certitudes, against our omniscient humors, we must above all, by creating for ourselves *another* death, one that will be incompatible with our carrion carcasses, consent to the undemonstrable, to the idea that something exists . . .

Nothingness may well have been more convenient. How difficult it is to *dissolve* oneself in Being!

A NOTE ON THE AUTHOR

E. M. Cioran writes: "I was born on the 8th April 1911 in Rasinari, a village in the Carpathians, where my teacher was a Greek Orthodox priest. From 1920 to 1928 I attended the Sibiu grammar school. From 1929 to 1931 I studied at the Faculty of Arts at Bucharest University. Post-graduate studies in philosophy until 1936. In 1937 I came to Paris with a scholarship from the French Institute in Bucharest and have been living here ever since. I have no nationality—the best possible status for an intellectual. On the other hand, I have not disowned my Rumanian origins; had I to choose a country, I would still choose my own. Before the war I published various essays in Rumanian of a more or less philosophical nature. I only began writing in French in about 1947. It was the hardest experience I have ever undergone. This precise, highly disciplined, and exacting language seemed as restrictive to me as a straitjacket. Even now I must confess that I do not feel completely at ease with it. It is this feeling of uneasiness which has led me to ponder the problem of style and the very *anomaly* of writing. All my books are more or less autobiographical—a rather abstract form of autobiography, I admit." Since 1949 M. Cioran has written A *Short History of Decay, The Trouble with Being Born, Drawn and Quartered, History and Utopia, Syllogismes de l'Amertume, Joseph de Maistre, La Chute dans le Temps.*